Set 2250

P9-DWZ-129

THE YALE SHAKESPEARE

EDITED BY

WILBUR L. CROSS   TUCKER BROOKE

PUBLISHED UNDER THE DIRECTION
OF THE
DEPARTMENT OF ENGLISH, YALE UNIVERSITY,
ON THE FUND
GIVEN TO THE YALE UNIVERSITY PRESS IN 1917
BY THE MEMBERS OF THE
KINGSLEY TRUST ASSOCIATION
(SCROLL AND KEY SOCIETY OF YALE COLLEGE)
TO COMMEMORATE THE SEVENTY-FIFTH ANNIVERSARY
OF THE FOUNDING OF THE SOCIETY

·: *The Yale Shakespeare* :·

THE COMEDY OF ERRORS

EDITED BY

ROBERT DUDLEY FRENCH

NEW HAVEN · YALE UNIVERSITY PRESS
LONDON · GEOFFREY CUMBERLEGE
OXFORD UNIVERSITY PRESS

COPYRIGHT, 1926
BY YALE UNIVERSITY PRESS
Printed in the United States of America

———

First published, March, 1926
Second printing, April, 1954

All rights reserved to the editorial contribu-
tions to this edition, which may not be reproduced, in whole or in part, in any form, except
by written permission from the publishers.

CONTENTS

The facsimile opposite reproduces, from a copy in the Library of Yale University, the frontispiece to 'The Comedy of Errors' in Rowe's edition of Shakespeare (1709). The scene depicted is Adriana's appeal to the Duke before the Abbey (V. i. 128 ff.). All characters are in Queen Anne dress.

p. 274

[DRAMATIS PERSONÆ

Solinus, *Duke of Ephesus*
Ægeon, *a Merchant of Syracuse*

Antipholus *of Ephesus,*
Antipholus *of Syracuse,* } *Twin Brothers, and sons to Ægeon and Æmilia, but unknown to each other*

Dromio *of Ephesus,*
Dromio *of Syracuse,* } *Twin Brothers, and slaves to the two Antipholuses*

Balthazar, *a Merchant*
Angelo, *a Goldsmith*
A Merchant, *Friend to Antipholus of Syracuse*
A Second Merchant, *to whom Angelo is a debtor*
Dr. Pinch, *a Schoolmaster, and a Conjurer*

Æmilia, *Wife to Ægeon, an Abbess at Ephesus*
Adriana, *Wife to Antipholus of Ephesus*
Luciana, *Sister to Adriana*
Luce, *Servant to Adriana*
A Courtesan

Gaoler, Officers, and other Attendants

Scene: *Ephesus.*]

Dramatis Personæ. First given by Rowe, 1709.

The Comedy of Errors

ACT FIRST

Scene One

[A Hall in the Duke's Palace]

*Enter the Duke of Ephesus, with the Merchant
    [Ægeon] of Syracusa, Gaoler, and other at-
    tendants.*

Merch. Proceed, Solinus, to procure my fall,
And by the doom of death end woes and all.
    Duke. Merchant of Syracusa, plead no more.
I am not partial to infringe our laws: **4**
The enmity and discord which of late
Sprung from the rancorous outrage of your duke
To merchants, our well-dealing countrymen,
Who, wanting guilders to redeem their lives,   **8**
Have seal'd his rigorous statutes with their bloods,
Excludes all pity from our threat'ning looks.
For, since the mortal and intestine jars
'Twixt thy seditious countrymen and us,   **12**
It hath in solemn synods been decreed,
Both by the Syracusians and ourselves,
To admit no traffic to our adverse towns:
Nay, more, if any, born at Ephesus,   **16**
Be seen at Syracusian marts and fairs;
Again, if any Syracusian born
Come to the bay of Ephesus: he dies,
His goods confiscate to the duke's dispose;   **20**

---

4 partial: *enough inclined in your behalf*   8 guilders: *money; cf. n.*
11 intestine; *cf. n.*   14 Syracusians: *i.e. Syracusans*
20 confiscate: *confiscated*   dispose: *disposal*

Unless a thousand marks be levied,
To quit the penalty and to ransom him.
Thy substance, valu'd at the highest rate,
Cannot amount unto a hundred marks;   24
Therefore, by law thou art condemn'd to die.

    Merch. Yet this my comfort: when your words are
       done,
My woes end likewise with the evening sun.

    Duke. Well, Syracusian, say, in brief the cause   28
Why thou departedst from thy native home,
And for what cause thou cam'st to Ephesus.

    Merch. A heavier task could not have been impos'd
Than I to speak my griefs unspeakable: 32
Yet, that the world may witness that my end
Was wrought by nature, not by vile offence,
I'll utter what my sorrow gives me leave.
In Syracusa was I born, and wed   36
Unto a woman, happy but for me,
And by me too, had not our hap been bad.
With her I liv'd in joy: our wealth increas'd
By prosperous voyages I often made   40
To Epidamnum; till my factor's death,
And the great care of goods at random left,
Drew me from kind embracements of my spouse;
From whom my absence was not six months old,   44
Before herself,—almost at fainting under
The pleasing punishment that women bear,—
Had made provision for her following me,
And soon and safe arrived where I was.   48
There had she not been long but she became
A joyful mother of two goodly sons;
And, which was strange, the one so like the other,

21 marks: *a mark was worth 13s. 4d., about $3.35*
34 nature: *natural affection; cf. n.*
41 Epidamnum; *cf. n.*   factor's: *agent's*

As could not be distinguish'd but by names.   52
That very hour, and in the self-same inn,
A meaner woman was delivered
Of such a burthen, male twins, both alike.
Those,—for their parents were exceeding poor,—   56
I bought, and brought up to attend my sons.
My wife, not meanly proud of two such boys,
Made daily motions for our home return:
Unwilling I agreed.   Alas! too soon   60
We came aboard.
A league from Epidamnum had we sail'd,
Before the always-wind-obeying deep
Gave any tragic instance of our harm: 64
But longer did we not retain much hope;
For what obscured light the heavens did grant
Did but convey unto our fearful minds
A doubtful warrant of immediate death;   68
Which, though myself would gladly have embrac'd,
Yet the incessant weepings of my wife,
Weeping before for what she saw must come,
And piteous plainings of the pretty babes,   72
That mourn'd for fashion, ignorant what to fear,
Forc'd me to seek delays for them and me.
And this it was, for other means was none:
The sailors sought for safety by our boat,   76
And left the ship, then sinking-ripe, to us:
My wife, more careful for the latter-born,
Had fasten'd him unto a small spare mast,
Such as seafaring men provide for storms;   80
To him one of the other twins was bound,

52 As: *that they*   54 meaner: *of lower rank*
58 meanly: *moderately*   59 motions: *proposals*
64 instance: *indication*   67 fearful: *frightened*
68 doubtful: *dreadful*   72 plainings: *wailings*
73 for fashion: *from imitation of others*
77 sinking-ripe: *on the point of sinking*   78 latter-born; *cf. n.*

Whilst I had been like heedful of the other.
The children thus dispos'd, my wife and I,
Fixing our eyes on whom our care was fix'd,   84
Fasten'd ourselves at either end the mast;
And floating straight, obedient to the stream,
Was carried towards Corinth, as we thought.
At length the sun, gazing upon the earth,   88
Dispers'd those vapours that offended us,
And, by the benefit of his wished light
The seas wax'd calm, and we discovered
Two ships from far making amain to us,   92
Of Corinth that, of Epidaurus this:
But ere they came,—O let me say no more!
Gather the sequel by that went before.

    Duke. Nay, forward, old man; do not break off so; 96
For we may pity, though not pardon thee.

    Merch. O, had the gods done so, I had not now
Worthily term'd them merciless to us!
For, ere the ships could meet by twice five leagues, 100
We were encounter'd by a mighty rock,
Which being violently borne upon,
Our helpful ship was splitted in the midst;
So that, in this unjust divorce of us   104
Fortune had left to both of us alike
What to delight in, what to sorrow for.
Her part, poor soul! seeming as burdened
With lesser weight, but not with lesser woe,   108
Was carried with more speed before the wind,
And in our sight they three were taken up
By fishermen of Corinth, as we thought.
At length, another ship had seiz'd on us;   112
And, knowing whom it was their hap to save,
Gave healthful welcome to their ship-wrack'd guests;

92 amain: *swiftly*   93 Epidaurus; *cf. n.*
95 that: *what*   114 healthful: *salutary*

And would have reft the fishers of their prey,
Had not their bark been very slow of sail;   116
And therefore homeward did they bend their course.
Thus have you heard me sever'd from my bliss,
That by misfortunes was my life prolong'd,
To tell sad stories of my own mishaps.   120

Duke. And, for the sake of them thou sorrowest for,
Do me the favour to dilate at full
What hath befall'n of them and thee till now.

Merch. My youngest boy, and yet my eldest care, 124
At eighteen years became inquisitive
After his brother; and importun'd me
That his attendant—so his case was like,
Reft of his brother, but retain'd his name—   128
Might bear him company in the quest of him;
Whom whilst I labour'd of a love to see,
I hazarded the loss of whom I lov'd.
Five summers have I spent in farthest Greece,   132
Roaming clean through the bounds of Asia,
And, coasting homeward, came to Ephesus;
Hopeless to find, yet loath to leave unsought
Or that or any place that harbours men.   136
But here must end the story of my life;
And happy were I in my timely death,
Could all my travels warrant me they live.

Duke. Hapless Ægeon, whom the fates have
        mark'd   140
To bear the extremity of dire mishap!
Now, trust me, were it not against our laws,
Against my crown, my oath, my dignity,
Which princes, would they, may not disannul,   144
My soul should sue as advocate for thee.

122 dilate: *narrate*   133 clean: *entirely*
136 Or . . . or: *either . . . or*   138 timely: *speedy*
139 warrant me: *give me assurance that* 144 disannul: *annul*

But though thou art adjudged to the death,
And passed sentence may not be recall'd
But to our honour's great disparagement,   148
Yet will I favour thee in what I can:
Therefore, merchant, I'll limit thee this day
To seek thy life by beneficial help.
Try all the friends thou hast in Ephesus;   152
Beg thou, or borrow, to make up the sum,
And live; if no, then thou art doom'd to die.
Gaoler, take him to thy custody.

    Gaol. I will, my lord.   156

    Merch. Hopeless and helpless doth Ægeon wend,
But to procrastinate his lifeless end.   *Exeunt.*

Scene Two

[*The Mart*]

*Enter Antipholus Erotes [of Syracuse], a Merchant,
and Dromio [of Syracuse].*

    Mer. Therefore, give out you are of Epidamnum,
Lest that your goods too soon be confiscate.
This very day, a Syracusian merchant
Is apprehended for arrival here;   4
And, not being able to buy out his life,
According to the statute of the town
Dies ere the weary sun set in the west.
There is your money that I had to keep.   8

    Ant. S. Go bear it to the Centaur, where we host,
And stay there, Dromio, till I come to thee.
Within this hour it will be dinner-time:
Till that, I'll view the manners of the town,   12

151 life; *cf. n.*   Scene Two, S. d. Antipholus Erotes; *cf. n.*
9 host: *lodge*

Peruse the traders, gaze upon the buildings,
And then return and sleep within mine inn,
For with long travel I am stiff and weary.
Get thee away.   16

 Dro. S. Many a man would take you at your word,
And go indeed, having so good a mean.   *Exit Dromio.*

 Ant. S. A trusty villain, sir, that very oft,
When I am dull with care and melancholy,   20
Lightens my humour with his merry jests.
What, will you walk with me about the town,
And then go to my inn and dine with me?

 Mer. I am invited, sir, to certain merchants,   24
Of whom I hope to make much benefit;
I crave your pardon. Soon at five o'clock,
Please you, I'll meet with you upon the mart,
And afterward consort you till bed-time: 28
My present business calls me from you now.

 Ant. S. Farewell till then: I will go lose myself,
And wander up and down to view the city.

 Mer. Sir, I commend you to your own content.   32
             [Exit.]

 Ant. S. He that commends me to mine own content,
Commends me to the thing I cannot get.
I to the world am like a drop of water
That in the ocean seeks another drop;   36
Who, falling there to find his fellow forth,
Unseen, inquisitive, confounds himself:
So I, to find a mother and a brother,
In quest of them, unhappy, lose myself.   40

    Enter Dromio of Ephesus.

Here comes the almanac of my true date.

13 Peruse: *observe* 18 mean: *means (the money entrusted to him)*
19 villain: *fellow*   26 Soon at: *about*
28 consort you: *keep you company*
38 confounds himself: *i.e. is lost* 41 almanac of my true date; *cf. n.*
37 forth: *out*

What now? How chance thou art return'd so soon?

   Dro. E. Return'd so soon! rather approach'd too
    late:

The capon burns, the pig falls from the spit,   44
The clock hath strucken twelve upon the bell;
My mistress made it one upon my cheek:
She is so hot because the meat is cold;
The meat is cold because you come not home;   48
You come not home because you have no stomach;
You have no stomach, having broke your fast;
But we, that know what 'tis to fast and pray,
Are penitent for your default to-day.   52

   Ant. S. Stop in your wind, sir: tell me this, I pray:
Where have you left the money that I gave you?

   Dro. E. O, sixpence, that I had o' Wednesday last
To pay the saddler for my mistress' crupper?   56
The saddler had it, sir; I kept it not.

   Ant. S. I am not in a sportive humour now.
Tell me, and dally not, where is the money?
We being strangers here, how dar'st thou trust   60
So great a charge from thine own custody?

   Dro. E. I pray you, jest, sir, as you sit at dinner.
I from my mistress come to you in post;
If I return, I shall be post indeed,   64
For she will score your fault upon my pate.
Methinks your maw, like mine, should be your clock
And strike you home without a messenger.

   Ant. S. Come, Dromio, come, these jests are out of
    season;   68
Reserve them till a merrier hour than this.
Where is the gold I gave in charge to thee?

   Dro. E. To me, sir? why, you gave no gold to me.

<hr />

45 twelve: *somewhat past the Elizabethan dinner hour*
49 stomach: *appetite*   52 penitent: *i.e. doing penance*
63 post: *haste; cf. n.*

Ant. S. Come on, sir knave, have done your fool-
　　ishness,　　　　　　　　　　　　　　　　72
And tell me how thou hast dispos'd thy charge.

Dro. E. My charge was but to fetch you from the
　　mart
Home to your house, the Phœnix, sir, to dinner:
My mistress and her sister stays for you.　　76

Ant. S. Now, as I am a Christian, answer me,
In what safe place you have bestow'd my money;
Or I shall break that merry sconce of yours
That stands on tricks when I am undispos'd.　80
Where is the thousand marks thou hadst of me?

Dro. E. I have some marks of yours upon my pate,
Some of my mistress' marks upon my shoulders,
But not a thousand marks between you both.　84
If I should pay your worship those again,
Perchance you will not bear them patiently.

Ant. S. Thy mistress' marks! what mistress, slave,
　　hast thou?

Dro. E. Your worship's wife, my mistress at the
　　Phœnix;　　　　　　　　　　　　　　　88
She that doth fast till you come home to dinner,
And prays that you will hie you home to dinner.

Ant. S. What! wilt thou flout me thus unto my face,
Being forbid? There, take you that, sir knave.　92
　　　　　　　　　　　　　　　[Strikes him.]

Dro. E. What mean you, sir? for God's sake, hold
　　your hands!
Nay, an you will not, sir, I'll take my heels.
　　　　　　　　　　　　　　　Exit Dromio Ep.

Ant. S. Upon my life, by some device or other
The villain is o'er-raught of all my money.　96

73 dispos'd: *disposed of*　　　　　　75 Phœnix; *cf. n.*
78 bestow'd: *deposited*　79 sconce: *head*　80 stands on: *insists on*
94 S. d. Ep.: *i.e. of Ephesus*　　　　96 o'er-raught: *cheated*

They say this town is full of cozenage;
As, nimble jugglers that deceive the eye,
Dark-working sorcerers that change the mind,
Soul-killing witches that deform the body,   100
Disguised cheaters, prating mountebanks,
And many such-like liberties of sin:
If it prove so, I will be gone the sooner.
I'll to the Centaur, to go seek this slave: 104
I greatly fear my money is not safe.   *Exit.*

ACT SECOND

Scene One

[*The House of Antipholus of Ephesus*]

*Enter Adriana, wife to Antipholus Sereptus, with
Luciana her Sister.*

Adr. Neither my husband nor the slave return'd,
That in such haste I sent to seek his master!
Sure, Luciana, it is two o'clock.

  Luc. Perhaps some merchant hath invited him,   4
And from the mart he's somewhere gone to dinner.
Good sister, let us dine and never fret.
A man is master of his liberty:
Time is their master, and, when they see time,   8
They'll go or come: if so, be patient, sister.

  Adr. Why should their liberty than ours be more?

  Luc. Because their business still lies out o' door.

  Adr. Look, when I serve him so, he takes it ill.   12

  Luc. O, know he is the bridle of your will.

  Adr. There's none but asses will be bridled so.

97 cozenage: *cheating*   102 liberties of sin: *sinful liberties, license*
II. i. S. d. Antipholus Sereptus; *cf. n.*

 Luc. Why, headstrong liberty is lash'd with woe.

There's nothing situate under heaven's eye   16

But hath his bound, in earth, in sea, in sky:

The beasts, the fishes, and the winged fowls,

Are their males' subjects and at their controls.

Men, more divine, the masters of all these,   20

Lords of the wide world, and wild wat'ry seas,

Indu'd with intellectual sense and souls,

Of more pre-eminence than fish and fowls,

Are masters to their females and their lords: 24

Then, let your will attend on their accords.

 Adr. This servitude makes you to keep unwed.

 Luc. Not this, but troubles of the marriage-bed.

 Adr. But, were you wedded, you would bear some
  sway.   28

 Luc. Ere I learn love, I'll practise to obey.

 Adr. How if your husband start some other where?

 Luc. Till he come home again, I would forbear.

 Adr. Patience unmov'd! no marvel though she
  pause;   32

They can be meek that have no other cause.

A wretched soul, bruis'd with adversity,

We bid be quiet when we hear it cry;

But were we burden'd with like weight of pain, 36

As much, or more we should ourselves complain:

So thou, that hast no unkind mate to grieve thee,

With urging helpless patience wouldst relieve me;

But, if thou live to see like right bereft,   40

This fool-begg'd patience in thee will be left.

 Luc. Well, I will marry one day, but to try.

Here comes your man; now is your husband nigh.

---

15 lash'd: *scourged; cf. n.*   17 his: *its*

30 some other where: *i.e. after some other woman*

33 other cause: *cause to be otherwise*

39 helpless: *unavailing*   41 fool-begg'd: *foolishly demanded*

Enter Dromio Eph.

Adr. Say, is your tardy master now at hand?　　44

　Dro. E. Nay, he's at two hands with me, and
that my two ears can witness.

　Adr. Say, didst thou speak with him? Know'st
thou his mind?

　Dro. E. Ay, ay, he told his mind upon mine ear.　48
Beshrew his hand, I scarce could understand it.

　Luc. Spake he so doubtfully, thou couldst not
feel his meaning?

　Dro. E. Nay, he struck so plainly, I could too 52
well feel his blows; and withal so doubtfully,
that I could scarce understand them.

　Adr. But say, I prithee, is he coming home?
It seems he hath great care to please his wife.　　56

　Dro. E. Why, mistress, sure my master is horn-mad.

　Adr. Horn-mad, thou villain!

　Dro. E. I mean not cuckold-mad; but, sure, he is
stark mad.
When I desir'd him to come home to dinner,　　60
He ask'd me for a thousand marks in gold:
''Tis dinner time,' quoth I; 'My gold!' quoth he:
'Your meat doth burn,' quoth I; 'My gold!' quoth he:
'Will you come home?' quoth I; 'My gold!' quoth he, 64
'Where is the thousand marks I gave thee, villain?'
'The pig,' quoth I, 'is burn'd;' 'My gold!' quoth he:
'My mistress, sir,'—quoth I; 'Hang up thy mistress!
I know not thy mistress; out on thy mistress!'　　68

　Luc. Quoth who?

　Dro. E. Quoth my master:
'I know,' quoth he, 'no house, no wife, no mistress.'
So that my errand, due unto my tongue,　　72
I thank him, I bear home upon my shoulders;

49 Beshrew: *ill luck to*　　　　　　57 horn-mad; *cf. n.*

For, in conclusion, he did beat me there.

    Adr. Go back again, thou slave, and fetch him home.

    Dro. E. Go back again, and be new beaten home? 76
For God's sake, send some other messenger.

    Adr. Back, slave, or I will break thy pate across.

    Dro. E. And he will bless that cross with other
      beating:
Between you, I shall have a holy head. 80

    Adr. Hence, prating peasant! fetch thy master home.

    Dro. E. Am I so round with you as you with me,
That like a football you do spurn me thus?
You spurn me hence, and he will spurn me hither: 84
If I last in this service, you must case me in leather.
                          [*Exit.*]

    Luc. Fie, how impatience loureth in your face!

    Adr. His company must do his minions grace,
Whilst I at home starve for a merry look. 88
Hath homely age the alluring beauty took
From my poor cheek? then, he hath wasted it:
Are my discourses dull? barren my wit?
If voluble and sharp discourse be marr'd, 92
Unkindness blunts it more than marble hard:
Do their gay vestments his affections bait?
That's not my fault; he's master of my state:
What ruins are in me that can be found 96
By him not ruin'd? then is he the ground
Of my defeatures. My decayed fair
A sunny look of his would soon repair;
But, too unruly deer, he breaks the pale 100
And feeds from home: poor I am but his stale.

    Luc. Self-harming jealousy! fie, beat it hence!

    Adr. Unfeeling fools can with such wrongs dispense.

---

82 round; *cf. n.*   85 case: *encase*   87 minions: *darlings*
97 ground: *cause*   98 defeatures: *disfigurements*   fair: *beauty*
101 stale: *dupe, laughing-stock*   103 dispense: *put u*

I know his eye doth homage otherwhere, 104
Or else what lets it but he would be here?
Sister, you know he promis'd me a chain:
Would that alone, alone he would detain,
So he would keep fair quarter with his bed! 108
I see, the jewel best enamelled
Will lose his beauty; yet the gold bides still
That others touch, and often touching will
Wear gold; and no man that hath a name, 112
By falsehood and corruption doth it shame.
Since that my beauty cannot please his eye,
I'll weep what's left away, and weeping die.
　　Luc. How many fond fools serve mad jealousy! 116
　　　　　　　　　　　　　　Exit [*with Adriana*].

Scene Two

[*A public Place*]

Enter Antipholus Erotes [*of Syracuse*].

　Ant. S. The gold I gave to Dromio is laid up
Safe at the Centaur; and the heedful slave
Is wander'd forth, in care to seek me out.
By computation, and mine host's report, 4
I could not speak with Dromio since at first
I sent him from the mart. See, here he comes.

　　　　　Enter Dromio Siracusia.

How now, sir! is your merry humour alter'd?
As you love strokes, so jest with me again. 8
You know no Centaur? You receiv'd no gold?
Your mistress sent to have me home to dinner?

105 lets: *hinders* 　　　　　108 keep fair quarter with: *be true to*
109-113 I see . . . shame; *cf. n.* 　　　116 fond: *doting*

My house was at the Phœnix? Wast thou mad,
That thus so madly thou didst answer me?   12

   Dro. S. What answer, sir? when spake I such a
    word?

   Ant. S. Even now, even here, not half an hour since.

   Dro. S. I did not see you since you sent me hence,
Home to the Centaur, with the gold you gave me.   16

   Ant. S. Villain, thou didst deny the gold's receipt,
And told'st me of a mistress and a dinner;
For which, I hope, thou felt'st I was displeas'd.

   Dro. S. I am glad to see you in this merry vein: 20
What means this jest? I pray you, master, tell me.

   Ant. S. Yea, dost thou jeer, and flout me in the teeth?
Think'st thou I jest? Hold, take thou that, and that.
                           Beats Dro.

   Dro. S. Hold, sir, for God's sake! now your jest is
    earnest: 24
Upon what bargain do you give it me?

   Ant. S. Because that I familiarly sometimes
Do use you for my fool, and chat with you,
Your sauciness will jest upon my love,   28
And make a common of my serious hours.
When the sun shines let foolish gnats make sport,
But creep in crannies when he hides his beams.
If you will jest with me, know my aspect,   32
And fashion your demeanour to my looks,
Or I will beat this method in your sconce.

   Dro. S. Sconce, call you it? so you would
    leave battering, I had rather have it a head: 36
    an you use these blows long, I must get a sconce
    for my head and insconce it too; or else I shall

24 earnest; *cf. n.*   29 *Cf. n.*
32 aspect: *countenance; cf. n.*   37 sconce: *helmet; cf. n.*
38 insconce: *fortify*

seek my wit in my shoulders. But, I pray, sir,
why am I beaten? 40

Ant. S. Dost thou not know?

Dro. S. Nothing, sir, but that I am beaten.

Ant. S. Shall I tell you why?

Dro. S. Ay, sir, and wherefore; for they say 44
every why hath a wherefore.

Ant. S. Why, first,—for flouting me; and then,
wherefore,—

For urging it the second time to me.

Dro. S. Was there ever any man thus beaten out of
season, 48

When in the why and the wherefore is neither rime
nor reason?

Well, sir, I thank you.

Ant. S. Thank me, sir? for what?

Dro. S. Marry, sir, for this something that 52
you gave me for nothing.

Ant. S. I'll make you amends next, to give
you nothing for something. But say, sir, is it
dinner-time? 56

Dro. S. No, sir: I think the meat wants that
I have.

Ant. S. In good time, sir; what's that?

Dro. S. Basting. 60

Ant. S. Well, sir, then 'twill be dry.

Dro. S. If it be, sir, I pray you eat none of it.

Ant. S. Your reason?

Dro. S. Lest it make you choleric, and pur- 64
chase me another dry basting.

Ant. S. Well, sir, learn to jest in good time:
there's a time for all things.

59 In good time: *forsooth*   64 choleric: *irascible; cf. n.*
65 dry basting: *severe beating*

Dro. S. I durst have denied that, before you 68
were so choleric.

Ant. S. By what rule, sir?

Dro. S. Marry, sir, by a rule as plain as the
plain bald pate of Father Time himself.   72

Ant. S. Let's hear it.

Dro. S. There's no time for a man to recover
his hair that grows bald by nature.

Ant. S. May he not do it by fine and reco- 76
very?

Dro. S. Yes, to pay a fine for a periwig and
recover the lost hair of another man.

Ant. S. Why is Time such a niggard of hair, 80
being, as it is, so plentiful an excrement?

Dro. S. Because it is a blessing that he be-
stows on beasts: and what he hath scanted men
in hair, he hath given them in wit.   84

Ant. S. Why, but there's many a man hath
more hair than wit.

Dro. S. Not a man of those but he hath the
wit to lose his hair.   88

Ant. S. Why, thou didst conclude hairy men
plain dealers without wit.

Dro. S. The plainer dealer, the sooner lost:
yet he loseth it in a kind of jollity.   92

Ant. S. For what reason?

Dro. S. For two; and sound ones too.

Ant. S. Nay, not sound, I pray you.

Dro. S. Sure ones then.   96

Ant. S. Nay, not sure, in a thing falsing.

Dro. S. Certain ones, then.

Ant. S. Name them.

71 Marry: *originally an oath by the Virgin Mary*
76 fine and recovery: *a legal term; cf. n.*
81 excrement: *outgrowth*   87, 88 he hath . . . hair; *cf. n.*
92 jollity; *cf. n.*   97 falsing: *deceptive*

Dro. S. The one, to save the money that he 100
spends in tiring; the other, that at dinner they
should not drop in his porridge.

Ant. S. You would all this time have proved
there is no time for all things.   104

Dro. S. Marry, and did, sir; namely, no time
to recover hair lost by nature.

Ant. S. But your reason was not substantial,
why there is no time to recover.   108

Dro. S. Thus I mend it: Time himself is bald,
and therefore to the world's end will have bald
followers.

Ant. S. I knew 'twould be a bald conclusion. 112
But soft! who wafts us yonder?

Enter Adriana and Luciana.

Adr. Ay, ay, Antipholus, look strange, and frown:
Some other mistress hath thy sweet aspects;
I am not Adriana, nor thy wife.   116
The time was once when thou unurg'd wouldst vow
That never words were music to thine ear,
That never object pleasing in thine eye,
That never touch well welcome to thy hand,   120
That never meat sweet-savour'd in thy taste,
Unless I spake, or look'd, or touch'd, or carv'd to thee.
How comes it now, my husband, O, how comes it,
That thou art then estranged from thyself?   124
Thyself I call it, being strange to me,
That, undividable, incorporate,
Am better than thy dear self's better part.
Ah, do not tear away thyself from me!   128
For know, my love, as easy mayst thou fall
A drop of water in the breaking gulf,

101 tiring: *dressing the hair; cf. n.*   112 bald: *senseless*
113 wafts: *beckons*   127 better part: *soul, spirit*   129 fall: *let fall*

And take unmingled thence that drop again,
Without addition or diminishing,   132
As take from me thyself and not me too.
How dearly would it touch thee to the quick,
Shouldst thou but hear I were licentious,
And that this body, consecrate to thee,   136
By ruffian lust should be contaminate!
Wouldst thou not spit at me and spurn at me,
And hurl the name of husband in my face,
And tear the stain'd skin off my harlot-brow,   140
And from my false hand cut the wedding-ring
And break it with a deep-divorcing vow?
I know thou canst; and therefore, see thou do it.
I am possess'd with an adulterate blot;   144
My blood is mingled with the crime of lust:
For if we two be one and thou play false,
I do digest the poison of thy flesh,
Being strumpeted by thy contagion.   148
Keep then fair league and truce with thy true bed;
I live distain'd, thou undishonoured.

   Ant. S. Plead you to me, fair dame? I know you not:
In Ephesus I am but two hours old,   152
As strange unto your town as to your talk;
Who, every word by all my wit being scann'd,
Wants wit in all one word to understand.

   Luc. Fie, brother! how the world is chang'd with
     you!   156
When were you wont to use my sister thus?
She sent for you by Dromio home to dinner.

   Ant. S. By Dromio?

   Dro. S. By me?   160

   Adr. By thee; and this thou didst return from him,
That he did buffet thee, and in his blows,

134 dearly: *grievously*   148 strumpeted: *made a strumpet*
150 distain'd: *stained; cf. n.*

Denied my house for his, me for his wife.

   Ant. S. Did you converse, sir, with this gentle-
     woman?　　　　　　　　　　　　　　　　　164

What is the course and drift of your compact?

   Dro. S. I, sir? I never saw her till this time.

   Ant. S. Villain, thou liest; for even her very words
Didst thou deliver to me on the mart.　　　　　168

   Dro. S. I never spake with her in all my life.

   Ant. S. How can she thus, then, call us by our names,
Unless it be by inspiration?

   Adr. How ill agrees it with your gravity　　　172
To counterfeit thus grossly with your slave,
Abetting him to thwart me in my mood!
Be it my wrong you are from me exempt,
But wrong not that wrong with a more contempt.　176
Come, I will fasten on this sleeve of thine:
Thou art an elm, my husband, I a vine,
Whose weakness, married to thy stronger state,
Makes me with thy strength to communicate:　　180
If aught possess thee from me, it is dross,
Usurping ivy, brier, or idle moss;
Who, all for want of pruning, with intrusion
Infect thy sap and live on thy confusion.　　　184

   Ant. S. To me she speaks; she moves me for her
     theme!

What, was I married to her in my dream?
Or sleep I now and think I hear all this?
What error drives our eyes and ears amiss?　　188
Until I know this sure uncertainty,
I'll entertain the offer'd fallacy.

---

174 mood: *anger*　　　　　　　　　　　175 exempt: *separated*
181 possess . . . me: *dispossess me of thee*
182 idle: *barren, unfruitful*　　　　　　　184 confusion: *ruin*
185 moves: *appeals to*　　　theme: *subject*
189 *Until I unravel this undeniable mystery*
190 entertain . . . fallacy: *accept the unreal situation*

Luc. Dromio, go bid the servants spread for dinner.

Dro. S. O, for my beads! I cross me for a sinner. 192

This is the fairy land: O spite of spites!

We talk with goblins, owls, and sprites:

If we obey them not, this will ensue,

They'll suck our breath, or pinch us black and blue. 196

Luc. Why prat'st thou to thyself and answer'st not?

Dromio, thou drone, thou snail, thou slug, thou sot!

Dro. S. I am transformed, master, am not I?

Ant. S. I think thou art, in mind, and so am I.   200

Dro. S. Nay, master, both in mind and in my shape.

Ant. S. Thou hast thine own form.

Dro. S.   No, I am an ape.

Luc. If thou art chang'd to aught, 'tis to an ass.

Dro. S. 'Tis true; she rides me, and I long for grass.   204

'Tis so, I am an ass; else it could never be

But I should know her as well as she knows me.

Adr. Come, come, no longer will I be a fool,

To put the finger in the eye and weep,   208

Whilst man and master laughs my woes to scorn.

Come, sir, to dinner. Dromio, keep the gate.

Husband, I'll dine above with you to-day,

And shrive you of a thousand idle pranks.   212

Sirrah, if any ask you for your master,

Say he dines forth, and let no creature enter.

Come, sister. Dromio, play the porter well.

Ant. S. Am I in earth, in heaven, or in hell?   216

Sleeping or waking? mad or well-advis'd?

Known unto these, and to myself disguis'd!

I'll say as they say, and persever so,

And in this mist at all adventures go.   220

192 beads: *rosary*   198 sot: *fool*
208 put . . . eye: *play the child*   209 laughs; *cf. n.*
212 shrive you: *call you to confession*   214 forth: *away from home*
217 well-advis'd: *in my right mind*

Dro. S. Master, shall I be porter at the gate?

Adr. Ay; and let none enter, lest I break your pate.

Luc. Come, come, Antipholus, we dine too late.

            [*Exeunt.*]

ACT THIRD

Scene One

[Before the House of Antipholus of Ephesus]

Enter Antipholus of Ephesus, his man Dromio, Angelo the Goldsmith, and Balthazar the Merchant.

Ant. E. Good Signior Angelo, you must excuse us all;
My wife is shrewish when I keep not hours;
Say that I linger'd with you at your shop
To see the making of her carkanet,   4
And that to-morrow you will bring it home.
But here's a villain, that would face me down
He met me on the mart, and that I beat him,
And charg'd him with a thousand marks in gold, 8
And that I did deny my wife and house.
Thou drunkard, thou, what didst thou mean by this?

Dro. E. Say what you will, sir, but I know what I
   know;
That you beat me at the mart, I have your hand to
   show: 12
If the skin were parchment and the blows you gave
   were ink,
Your own handwriting would tell you what I think.

Ant. E. I think thou art an ass.

Dro. E.   Marry, so it doth appear
By the wrongs I suffer and the blows I bear.   16

4 carkanet: *gold collar*
8 charg'd him with: *asked him to account for*

I should kick, being kick'd; and, being at that pass,
You would keep from my heels and beware of an ass.

   Ant. E. You are sad, Signior Balthazar: pray God,
     our cheer
May answer my good will and your good welcome
   here.   20

   Bal. I hold your dainties cheap, sir, and your wel-
     come dear.

   Ant. E. O, Signior Balthazar, either at flesh or fish,
A table-full of welcome makes scarce one dainty dish.

   Bal. Good meat, sir, is common; that every churl
     affords.   24

   Ant. E. And welcome more common, for that's noth-
     ing but words.

   Bal. Small cheer and great welcome makes a merry
     feast.

   Ant. E. Ay, to a niggardly host and more sparing
     guest:
But though my cates be mean, take them in good
   part;   28
Better cheer may you have, but not with better heart.
But soft! my door is lock'd. Go bid them let us in.

   Dro. E. Maud, Bridget, Marian, Cicely, Gillian,
     Ginn!

   Dro. S. [*Within.*] Mome, malt-horse, capon, cox-
     comb, idiot, patch!   32
Either get thee from the door or sit down at the hatch.
Dost thou conjure for wenches, that thou call'st for
   such store,
When one is one too many? Go, get thee from the
   door.

28 cates: *dainties*   31 Gillian: *Juliana*   Ginn: *Jenny* (?)
32 Mome: *buffoon*   malt-horse: *brewer's horse, hence a term of*
   contempt   33 hatch: *half-door, wicket*

Dro. E. What patch is made our porter?—My
    master stays in the street.   36

Dro. S. [*Within.*] Let him walk from whence he
    came, lest he catch cold on's feet.

Ant. E. Who talks within there? ho, open the door!

Dro. S. [*Within.*] Right, sir; I'll tell you when, an
    you'll tell me wherefore.

Ant. E. Wherefore? for my dinner: I have not din'd
    to-day.   40

Dro. S. Nor to-day here you must not; come again
    when you may.

Ant. E. What art thou that keep'st me out from the
    house I owe?

Dro. S. [*Within.*] The porter for this time, sir, and
    my name is Dromio.

Dro. E. O villain, thou hast stolen both mine office
    and my name!   44

The one ne'er got me credit, the other mickle blame.

If thou hadst been Dromio to-day in my place,

Thou wouldst have chang'd thy face for a name, or thy
    name for an ass.

Luce. [*Within.*] What a coil is there, Dromio! who
    are those at the gate?   48

Dro. E. Let my master in, Luce.

Luce. [*Within.*] Faith, no; he comes too late;

And so tell your master.

Dro. E.   O Lord! I must laugh.

Have at you with a proverb: Shall I set in my staff?

Luce. [*Within.*] Have at you with another: that's—
    when? can you tell?   52

Dro. S. [*Within.*] If thy name be call'd Luce,—
    Luce, thou hast answer'd him well.

---

37 on's: *in his*   42 owe: *own*   45 mickle: *much*
46, 47 *Cf. n.*   48 S. d. Within; *cf. n.*   coil: *fuss*
51 set in my staff: '*make myself at home*' (?)
52 when? can you tell; *cf. n.*

Ant. E. Do you hear, you minion? you'll let us in,
I trow?

Luce. [*Within.*] I thought to have ask'd you.

Dro. S. [*Within.*]   And you said, no.

Dro. E. So come, help: well struck! there was blow
for blow.   56

Ant. E. Thou baggage, let me in.

Luce. [*Within.*]   Can you tell for whose sake?

Dro. E. Master, knock the door hard.

Luce. [*Within.*]   Let him knock till it ache.

Ant. E. You'll cry for this, minion, if I beat the
door down.

Luce. [*Within.*] What needs all that, and a pair of
stocks in the town?   60

Adr. [*Within.*] Who is that at the door that keeps
all this noise?

Dro. S. [*Within.*] By my troth your town is
troubled with unruly boys.

Ant. E. Are you there, wife? you might have come
before.

Adr. [*Within.*] Your wife, sir knave! go, get you
from the door.   64

Dro. E. If you went in pain, master, this 'knave'
would go sore.

Ang. Here is neither cheer, sir, nor welcome: we
would fain have either.

Bal. In debating which was best, we shall part with
neither.

Dro. E. They stand at the door, master: bid them
welcome hither.   68

Ant. E. There is something in the wind, that we cannot get in.

Dro. E. You would say so, master, if your garments
were thin.

Your cake here is warm within; you stand here in the
cold:

It would make a man mad as a buck to be so bought and
sold. 72

Ant. E. Go fetch me something: I'll break ope the
gate.

Dro. S. [*Within.*] Break any breaking here, and I'll
break your knave's pate.

Dro. E. A man may break a word with you, sir, and
words are but wind:

Ay, and break it in your face, so he break it not behind. 76

Dro. S. [*Within.*] It seems thou wantest breaking:
out upon thee, hind!

Dro. E. Here's too much 'out upon thee!' I pray
thee, let me in.

Dro. S. [*Within.*] Ay, when fowls have no feathers,
and fish have no fin.

Ant. E. Well, I'll break in. Go borrow me a crow. 80

Dro. E. A crow without feather? Master, mean you
so?

For a fish without a fin, there's a fowl without a
feather:

If a crow help us in, sirrah, we'll pluck a crow together.

Ant. E. Go get thee gone: fetch me an iron crow. 84

Bal. Have patience, sir; O let it not be so!

Herein you war against your reputation,

And draw within the compass of suspect

The unviolated honour of your wife. 88

Once this,—your long experience of her wisdom,

---

72 bought and sold: *imposed upon*   77 hind: *slave*
80 crow: *crowbar*   87 draw . . . suspect: *bring into suspicion*
89 Once this: *once for all, in short*

Her sober virtue, years, and modesty,
Plead on her part some cause to you unknown;
And doubt not, sir, but she will well excuse   92
Why at this time the doors are made against you.
Be rul'd by me: depart in patience,
And let us to the Tiger all to dinner;
And about evening come yourself alone,   96
To know the reason of this strange restraint.
If by strong hand you offer to break in
Now in the stirring passage of the day,
A vulgar comment will be made of it,   100
And that supposed by the common rout
Against your yet ungalled estimation,
That may with foul intrusion enter in
And dwell upon your grave when you are dead;   104
For slander lives upon succession,
For ever hous'd where it gets possession.

   Ant. E. You have prevail'd: I will depart in quiet,
And, in despite of mirth, mean to be merry.   108
I know a wench of excellent discourse,
Pretty and witty, wild and yet too gentle:
There will we dine. This woman that I mean,
My wife—but I protest, without desert—   112
Hath oftentimes upbraided me withal:
To her will we to dinner. [*To Angelo.*] Get you home,
And fetch the chain; by this I know 'tis made:
Bring it, I pray you, to the Porpentine;   116
For there's the house: that chain will I bestow,
Be it for nothing but to spite my wife,
Upon mine hostess there. Good sir, make haste.

93 made: *fastened*   99 stirring passage: *hour of busy traffic*
100 vulgar: *public*   101 supposed: *conjectured*
102 ungalled: *unblemished*   105 *Cf. n.*
108 in despite of mirth: *i.e. though I do not feel like being merry*
112 desert: *i.e. my deserving it*
116 Porpentine: *porcupine (house-sign)*

Since mine own doors refuse to entertain me,   120
I'll knock elsewhere, to see if they'll disdain me.
  Ang. I'll meet you at that place some hour hence.
  Ant. E. Do so. This jest shall cost me some expense.
                              Exeunt.

Scene Two

[*The Same*]

Enter Luciana with Antipholus of Syracusia.

Luc. And may it be that you have quite forgot
  A husband's office? Shall, Antipholus,
Even in the spring of love, thy love-springs rot?
  Shall love, in building, grow so ruinous?   4
If you did wed my sister for her wealth,
  Then, for her wealth's sake use her with more kind-
      ness:
Or, if you like elsewhere, do it by stealth;
  Muffle your false love with some show of blindness: 8
Let not my sister read it in your eye;
  Be not thy tongue thy own shame's orator;
Look sweet, speak fair, become disloyalty;
  Apparel vice like virtue's harbinger;   12
Bear a fair presence, though your heart be tainted;
  Teach sin the carriage of a holy saint;
Be secret-false: what need she be acquainted?
  What simple thief brags of his own attaint?   16
'Tis double wrong to truant with your bed,
  And let her read it in thy looks at board:
Shame hath a bastard fame, well managed;
  Ill deeds are doubled with an evil word.   20

Scene Two S. d. Luciana; *cf. n.*   3 love-springs: *shoots of love*
4 in building: *even before completely built*
11 become disloyalty; *cf. n.*   15 what: *why*
16 attaint: *disgrace*

Alas, poor women! make us but believe,
    Being compact of credit, that you love us;
Though others have the arm, show us the sleeve;
    We in your motion turn, and you may move us.   24
Then, gentle brother, get you in again;
    Comfort my sister, cheer her, call her wife:
'Tis holy sport to be a little vain,
    When the sweet breath of flattery conquers strife. 28
Ant. S. Sweet mistress,—what your name is else, I
      know not,
    Nor by what wonder you do hit of mine,—
Less in your knowledge and your grace you show not
    Than our earth's wonder; more than earth divine. 32
Teach me, dear creature, how to think and speak:
    Lay open to my earthy-gross conceit,
Smother'd in errors, feeble, shallow, weak,
    The folded meaning of your words' deceit.   36
Against my soul's pure truth why labour you
    To make it wander in an unknown field?
Are you a god? would you create me new?
    Transform me, then, and to your power I'll yield.   40
But if that I am I, then well I know
    Your weeping sister is no wife of mine,
Nor to her bed no homage do I owe:
    Far more, far more, to you do I decline.   44
O train me not, sweet mermaid, with thy note,
    To drown me in thy sister flood of tears!
Sing, siren, for thyself, and I will dote:
    Spread o'er the silver waves thy golden hairs,   48
And as a bed I'll take them and there lie;
    And in that glorious supposition think
He gains by death that hath such means to die:

22 compact of credit: *wholly made up of credulity*
27 vain: *extravagant in language*
34 conceit: *understanding*
44 decline: *incline*

30 hit of: *guess*
36 folded: *concealed*
45 train: *entice*

Let Love, being light, be drowned if she sink!   52
Luc. What, are you mad, that you do reason so?
Ant. S. Not mad, but mated; how, I do not know.
Luc. It is a fault that springeth from your eye.
Ant. S. For gazing on your beams, fair sun, being
by.   56
Luc. Gaze where you should, and that will clear
your sight.
Ant. S. As good to wink, sweet love, as look on night.
Luc. Why call you me love? call my sister so.
Ant. S. Thy sister's sister.
Luc.   That's my sister.
Ant. S.   No; 60
It is thyself, mine own self's better part;
Mine eye's clear eye, my dear heart's dearer heart;
My food, my fortune, and my sweet hope's aim,
My sole earth's heaven, and my heaven's claim.   64
Luc. All this my sister is, or else should be.
Ant. S. Call thyself sister, sweet, for I aim thee.
Thee will I love and with thee lead my life:
Thou hast no husband yet nor I no wife.   68
Give me thy hand.
Luc.   O, soft, sir! hold you still:
I'll fetch my sister, to get her good will.   *Exit.*

Enter Dromio Siracusia.

Ant. S. Why, how now, Dromio! where run'st
thou so fast?   72
Dro. S. Do you know me, sir? am I Dromio?
am I your man? am I myself?
Ant. S. Thou art Dromio, thou art my man,
thou art thyself.   76

---

52 *Cf. n.*   53 reason: *argue*
54 mated: *bewildered; also, furnished* **with a mate**
56 being by: *when you are near*   58 wink: *close the eyes*
64 *Cf. n.*   66 aim: *mean*

Dro. S. I am an ass, I am a woman's man and besides myself.

Ant. S. What woman's man? and how besides thyself?   80

Dro. S. Marry, sir, besides myself, I am due to a woman; one that claims me, one that haunts me, one that will have me.

Ant. S. What claim lays she to thee?   84

Dro. S. Marry, sir, such claim as you would lay to your horse; and she would have me as a beast: not that, I being a beast, she would have me; but that she, being a very beastly 88 creature, lays claim to me.

Ant. S. What is she?

Dro. S. A very reverent body; aye, such a one as a man may not speak of, without he say, 92 'Sir-reverence.'   I have but lean luck in the match, and yet is she a wondrous fat marriage.

Ant. S. How dost thou mean a fat marriage?   96

Dro. S. Marry, sir, she's the kitchen-wench, and all grease; and I know not what use to put her to, but to make a lamp of her and run from her by her own light. I warrant her rags and 100 the tallow in them will burn a Poland winter; if she lives till doomsday, she'll burn a week longer than the whole world.

Ant. S. What complexion is she of?   104

Dro. S. Swart, like my shoe, but her face nothing like so clean kept: for why she sweats; a man may go over shoes in the grime of it.

Ant. S. That's a fault that water will mend.   108

93 'Sir-reverence'; *cf. n.*   lean: *poor*   105 Swart: *swarthy*
106 for why: *because*

Dro. S. No, sir, 'tis in grain; Noah's flood could not do it.

Ant. S. What's her name?

Dro. S. Nell, sir; but her name and three 112 quarters,—that's an ell and three-quarters,— will not measure her from hip to hip.

Ant. S. Then she bears some breadth?

Dro. S. No longer from head to foot than 116 from hip to hip: she is spherical, like a globe; I could find out countries in her.

Ant. S. In what part of her body stands Ireland? 120

Dro. S. Marry, sir, in her buttocks: I found it out by the bogs.

Ant. S. Where Scotland?

Dro. S. I found it by the barrenness; hard 124 in the palm of the hand.

Ant. S. Where France?

Dro. S. In her forehead, armed and reverted, making war against her heir. 128

Ant. S. Where England?

Dro. S. I looked for the chalky cliffs, but I could find no whiteness in them; but I guess it stood in her chin, by the salt rheum that ran 132 between France and it.

Ant. S. Where Spain?

Dro. S. Faith, I saw it not; but I felt it hot in her breath. 136

Ant. S. Where America, the Indies?

Dro. S. O, sir! upon her nose, all o'er embellished with rubies, carbuncles, sapphires, declining their rich aspect to the hot breath of 140

109 in grain: *fast dyed*   127, 128 armed . . . heir; *cf. n.*
131 them: *i.e. her teeth*

Spain, who sent whole armadoes of carracks to
be ballast at her nose.

    Ant. S. Where stood Belgia, the Netherlands?

    Dro. S. O, sir! I did not look so low. To 144
conclude, this drudge, or diviner, laid claim to
me; call'd me Dromio; swore I was assured to
her; told me what privy marks I had about me,
as the mark of my shoulder, the mole in my 148
neck, the great wart on my left arm, that I,
amazed, ran from her as a witch:

And, I think, if my breast had not been made of faith
    and my heart of steel,

She had transform'd me to a curtal dog and made me
    turn i' the wheel.   152

    Ant. S. Go hie thee presently post to the road:

An if the wind blow any way from shore,

I will not harbour in this town to-night:

If any bark put forth, come to the mart,   156

Where I will walk till thou return to me.

If every one knows us and we know none,

'Tis time, I think, to trudge, pack, and be gone.

    Dro. S. As from a bear a man would run for life, 160
So fly I from her that would be my wife.   *Exit.*

    Ant. S. There's none but witches do inhabit here,

And therefore 'tis high time that I were hence.

She that doth call me husband, even my soul   164

Doth for a wife abhor; but her fair sister,

Possess'd with such a gentle sovereign grace,

Of such enchanting presence and discourse,

Hath almost made me traitor to myself: 168

---

141 armadoes: *fleets*   carracks: *large merchant ships*
142 ballast: *ballasted, loaded*   145 diviner: *sorceress*
146 assured: *betrothed*   149 that: *so that*
152 curtal: *having a docked tail*   turn i' the wheel; *cf. n.*
153 presently: *immediately*   road: *harbor*

But, lest myself be guilty to self-wrong,
I'll stop mine ears against the mermaid's song.

Enter Angelo with the chain.

Ang. Master Antipholus!

Ant. S. Ay, that's my name. 172

Ang. I know it well, sir: lo, here is the chain.
I thought to have ta'en you at the Porpentine:
The chain unfinish'd made me stay thus long.

Ant. S. What is your will that I shall do with
this? 176

Ang. What please yourself, sir: I have made it for
you.

Ant. S. Made it for me, sir! I bespoke it not.

Ang. Not once, nor twice, but twenty times you have.
Go home with it and please your wife withal; 180
And soon at supper-time I'll visit you,
And then receive my money for the chain.

Ant. S. I pray you, sir, receive the money now,
For fear you ne'er see chain nor money more. 184

Ang. You are a merry man, sir: fare you well.

Exit.

Ant. S. What I should think of this, I cannot tell:
But this I think, there's no man is so vain
That would refuse so fair an offer'd chain. 188
I see, a man here needs not live by shifts,
When in the streets he meets such golden gifts.
I'll to the mart, and there for Dromio stay:
If any ship put out, then straight away. *Exit.* 192

169 to: *of*   187 vain: *silly*

ACT FOURTH

Scene One

[A Public Place]

Enter a [second] Merchant, Goldsmith [Angelo],
and an Officer.

Mer. You know since Pentecost the sum is due,
And since I have not much importun'd you;
Nor now I had not, but that I am bound
To Persia, and want guilders for my voyage: 4
Therefore make present satisfaction,
Or I'll attach you by this officer.

Ang. Even just the sum that I do owe to you
Is growing to me by Antipholus;   8
And in the instant that I met with you
He had of me a chain: at five o'clock
I shall receive the money for the same.
Pleaseth you walk with me down to his house,   12
I will discharge my bond, and thank you too.

Enter Antipholus Ephes. [and the Ephesian]
Dromio from the Courtesan's.

Off. That labour may you save: see where he comes.
Ant. E. While I go to the goldsmith's house, go thou
And buy a rope's end: that will I bestow   16
Among my wife and her confederates,
For locking me out of my doors by day.
But soft! I see the goldsmith. Get thee gone;
Buy thou a rope, and bring it home to me.   20
Dro. E. I buy a thousand pound a year! I buy a
rope!   *Exit Dromio.*

---

6 attach: *arrest*   8 growing: *accruing*
16 bestow: *employ*   21 I buy . . . year; *cf. n.*

Ant. E. A man is well holp up that trusts to you:
I promised your presence and the chain;
But neither chain nor goldsmith came to me.   24
Belike you thought our love would last too long,
If it were chain'd together, and therefore came not.

Ang. Saving your merry humour, here's the note
How much your chain weighs to the utmost carat,   28
The fineness of the gold, and chargeful fashion,
Which doth amount to three odd ducats more
Than I stand debted to this gentleman:
I pray you see him presently discharg'd,   32
For he is bound to sea and stays but for it.

Ant. E. I am not furnish'd with the present money;
Besides, I have some business in the town.
Good signior, take the stranger to my house,   36
And with you take the chain, and bid my wife
Disburse the sum on the receipt thereof:
Perchance I will be there as soon as you.

 Ang. Then, you will bring the chain to her yourself?   40

 Ant. E. No; bear it with you, lest I come not time
  enough.

 Ang. Well, sir, I will. Have you the chain about you?

Ant. E. An if I have not, sir, I hope you have,
Or else you may return without your money.   44

 Ang. Nay, come, I pray you, sir, give me the chain:
Both wind and tide stays for this gentleman,
And I, to blame, have held him here too long.

 Ant. E. Good Lord! you use this dalliance to excuse   48

Your breach of promise to the Porpentine.
I should have chid you for not bringing it,

22 holp: *helped*   25 Belike: *probably*
29 chargeful fashion: *costly workmanship* 31 debted: *indebted*
33 stays: *waits*   41 time: *in time*

But, like a shrew, you first begin to brawl.

Mer. The hour steals on; I pray you, sir, dispatch. 52

Ang. You hear how he importunes me: the chain!

Ant. E. Why, give it to my wife and fetch your
money.

Ang. Come, come, you know I gave it you even now.
Either send the chain or send me by some token.   56

Ant. E. Fie! now you run this humour out of breath.
Come, where's the chain? I pray you, let me see it.

Mer. My business cannot brook this dalliance.
Good sir, say whe'r you'll answer me or no: 60
If not, I'll leave him to the officer.

Ant. E. I answer you! what should I answer you?

Ang. The money that you owe me for the chain.

Ant. E. I owe you none till I receive the chain.   64

Ang. You know I gave it you half an hour since.

Ant. E. You gave me none: you wrong me much to
say so.

Ang. You wrong me more, sir, in denying it:
Consider how it stands upon my credit.   68

Mer. Well, officer, arrest him at my suit.

Off. I do;
And charge you in the duke's name to obey me.

Ang. This touches me in reputation.   72
Either consent to pay this sum for me,
Or I attach you by this officer.

Ant. E. Consent to pay thee that I never had!
Arrest me, foolish fellow, if thou dar'st.   76

Ang. Here is thy fee: arrest him, officer.
I would not spare my brother in this case,
If he should scorn me so apparently.

Off. I do arrest you, sir: you hear the suit.   80

---

56 send . . . token; *cf. n.*
60 whe'r: *whether*   answer me: *discharge the debt to me*
68 stands upon: *concerns*   79 apparently: *openly*

Ant. E. I do obey thee till I give thee bail.
But, sirrah, you shall buy this sport as dear
As all the metal in your shop will answer.

Ang. Sir, sir, I shall have law in Ephesus,   84
To your notorious shame, I doubt it not.

Enter Dromio Sira. from the Bay.

Dro. S. Master, there is a bark of Epidamnum
That stays but till her owner comes aboard,
And then she bears away. Our fraughtage, sir,   88
I have convey'd aboard, and I have bought
The oil, the balsamum, and aqua-vitæ.
The ship is in her trim; the merry wind
Blows fair from land; they stay for nought at all   92
But for their owner, master, and yourself.

Ant. E. How now! a madman! Why, thou peevish
         sheep,
What ship of Epidamnum stays for me?

Dro. S. A ship you sent me to, to hire waftage.   96

Ant. E. Thou drunken slave, I sent thee for a rope,
And told thee to what purpose, and what end.

Dro. S. You sent me for a rope's end as soon:
You sent me to the bay, sir, for a bark.   100

Ant. E. I will debate this matter at more leisure,
And teach your ears to list me with more heed.
To Adriana, villain, hie thee straight:
Give her this key, and tell her, in the desk   104
That's cover'd o'er with Turkish tapestry,
There is a purse of ducats: let her send it.
Tell her I am arrested in the street,
And that shall bail me. Hie thee, slave, be gone!   108

88 fraughtage: *freight*
90 balsamum: *balsam*   aqua-vitæ: *brandy*
91 in her trim: *rigged, ready to sail*
94 peevish: *foolish*   sheep; *cf. n.*
102 list: *listen to*   96 waftage: *passage*

On, officer, to prison till it come.

                     Exeunt [*all except Dromio*].

Dro. S. To Adriana! that is where we din'd,
Where Dowsabel did claim me for her husband:
She is too big, I hope, for me to compass.   112
Thither I must, although against my will,
For servants must their masters' minds fulfil.   *Exit.*

Scene Two

[A Room in the House of Antipholus of Ephesus]

Enter Adriana and Luciana.

Adr. Ah, Luciana, did he tempt thee so?
  Mightst thou perceive austerely in his eye
That he did plead in earnest? yea or no?
  Look'd he or red or pale? or sad or merrily?   4
What observation mad'st thou in this case
Of his heart's meteors tilting in his face?
  Luc. First he denied you had in him no right.
  Adr. He meant he did me none; the more my spite. 8
  Luc. Then swore he that he was a stranger here.
  Adr. And true he swore, though yet forsworn he
    were.
  Luc. Then pleaded I for you.
  Adr.   And what said he?
  Luc. That love I begg'd for you he begg'd of me.   12
  Adr. With what persuasion did he tempt thy love?
  Luc. With words that in an honest suit might move.
First, he did praise my beauty, then my speech.
  Adr. Didst speak him fair?
  Luc.   Have patience, I beseech. 16

111 Dowsabel; *cf. n.*
6 *Cf. n.*

2 austerely: *seriously*
8 spite: *vexation*

Adr. I cannot, nor I will not hold me still:

My tongue, though not my heart, shall have his will.

He is deformed, crooked, old and sere,

Ill-fac'd, worse bodied, shapeless everywhere;   20

Vicious, ungentle, foolish, blunt, unkind,

Stigmatical in making, worse in mind.

Luc. Who would be jealous, then, of such a one?

No evil lost is wail'd when it is gone.   24

Adr. Ah, but I think him better than I say,

And yet would herein others' eyes were worse.

Far from her nest the lapwing cries away:

My heart prays for him, though my tongue do curse.   28

Enter S[yracusan] Dromio.

Dro. S. Here, go: the desk! the purse! sweet, now, make haste.

Luc. How hast thou lost thy breath?

Dro. S.   By running fast.

Adr. Where is thy master, Dromio? is he well?

Dro. S. No, he's in Tartar limbo, worse than hell.   32

A devil in an everlasting garment hath him,

One whose hard heart is button'd up with steel;

A fiend, a fairy, pitiless and rough;

A wolf, nay, worse, a fellow all in buff;   36

A back-friend, a shoulder-clapper, one that countermands

The passages of alleys, creeks and narrow lands;

A hound that runs counter and yet draws dry-foot well;

18 his: *its*   19 sere: *withered*   20 shapeless: *misshapen*
22 Stigmatical: *branded by deformity*   27 *Cf. n.*
32 Tartar: *Tartarean, infernal*   limbo: *cant term for prison*
33 everlasting: *i.e. made of buff, a very durable material*
35 fairy; *cf. n.*
37 A back-friend, a shoulder-clapper; *cf. n.*   countermands: *prohibits*
38 creeks: *narrow winding passages*
39 counter; *cf. n.*   draws dry-foot: *traces the scent of the game*

One that, before the judgment, carries poor souls to
    hell.   40

  Adr. Why, man, what is the matter?

  Dro. S. I do not know the matter: he is 'rested on the
    case.

  Adr. What, is he arrested? tell me at whose suit.

  Dro. S. I know not at whose suit he is arrested
    well;   44

But he's in a suit of buff which 'rested him, that can I
    tell.

Will you send him, mistress, redemption, the money in
    his desk?

  Adr. Go fetch it, sister.—This I wonder at:

                        Exit Luciana.

That he, unknown to me, should be in debt: 48

Tell me, was he arrested on a band?

  Dro. S. Not on a band, but on a stronger thing:

A chain, a chain.   Do you not hear it ring?

  Adr. What, the chain?   52

  Dro. S. No, no, the bell: 'tis time that I were gone:

It was two ere I left him, and now the clock strikes one.

  Adr. The hours come back! that did I never hear.

  Dro. S. O yes; if any hour meet a sergeant, a' turns
    back for very fear.   56

  Adr. As if Time were in debt! how fondly dost thou
    reason!

  Dro. S. Time is a very bankrupt, and owes more
    than he's worth to season.

Nay, he's a thief too: have you not heard men say,

That Time comes stealing on by night and day?   60

If Time be in debt and theft, and a sergeant in the way,

Hath he not reason to turn back an hour in a day?

40 *Cf. n.*   42 on the case; *cf. n.*
49 band: *bond*   56 a': *he (it)*
57 fondly: *foolishly*   58 owes . . . season; *cf. n.*

Enter Luciana.

Adr. Go, Dromio: there's the money, bear it straight,

And bring thy master home immediately.   64

Come, sister: I am press'd down with conceit,—

Conceit, my comfort and my injury.

        Exit [*with Luciana and Dromio*].

Scene Three

[*A Public Place*]

Enter Antipholus Siracusia.

Ant. S. There's not a man I meet but doth salute me,

As if I were their well acquainted friend;

And every one doth call me by my name.

Some tender money to me; some invite me;   4

Some other give me thanks for kindnesses;

Some offer me commodities to buy:

Even now a tailor call'd me in his shop

And show'd me silks that he had bought for me,   8

And therewithal, took measure of my body.

Sure, these are but imaginary wiles,

And Lapland sorcerers inhabit here.

    Enter Dromio [*of*] *Syr*[*acuse*].

Dro. S. Master, here's the gold you sent me for.   12

What, have you got the picture of old Adam new apparelled?

    Ant. S. What gold is this?   What Adam dost thou mean?

    Dro. S. Not that Adam that kept the Paradise, but that Adam that keeps the prison: he 16

65 conceit: *imaginings*   11 Lapland sorcerers; *cf. n.*   13 *Cf. n.*

that goes in the calf's skin that was killed for the
Prodigal: he that came behind you, sir, like an
evil angel, and bid you forsake your liberty.

Ant. S. I understand thee not.   20

Dro. S. No? why, 'tis a plain case: he that
went, like a base-viol, in a case of leather; the
man, sir, that, when gentlemen are tired, gives
them a sob, and 'rests them; he, sir, that takes 24
pity on decayed men and gives them suits of
durance; he that sets up his rest to do more
exploits with his mace than a morris-pike.

Ant. S. What, thou meanest an officer?   28

Dro. S. Ay, sir, the sergeant of the band; he
that brings any man to answer it that breaks
his band; one that thinks a man always going
to bed, and says, 'God give you good rest!'   32

Ant. S. Well, sir, there rest in your foolery.
Is there any ship puts forth to-night? may we
be gone?

Dro. S. Why, sir, I brought you word an hour 36
since that the bark Expedition put forth to-
night; and then were you hindered by the
sergeant to tarry for the hoy Delay. Here are
the angels that you sent for to deliver you.   40

Ant. S. The fellow is distract, and so am I;
And here we wander in illusions:
Some blessed power deliver us from hence!

Enter a Courtesan.

Cour. Well met, well met, Master Antipholus.   44

17, 18 calf's skin . . . Prodigal; *cf. n.*
24 sob: *slight rest given a horse to recover its wind*
25, 26 suits of durance: *durable garments, i.e. prison dress*
26 sets up his rest: *stakes his all*
27 mace: *club carried by a bailiff or constable*   morris-pike: *Moorish*
27   *pike*
39 hoy: *a small vessel*
40 angels: *gold coins worth about ten shillings apiece*
41 distract: *distracted, mad*

I see, sir, you have found the goldsmith now:
Is that the chain you promis'd me to-day?

Ant. S. Satan, avoid! I charge thee tempt me not!

Dro. S. Master, is this Mistress Satan? 48

Ant. S. It is the devil.

Dro. S. Nay, she is worse, she is the devil's dam, and here she comes in the habit of a light wench: and thereof comes that the wenches say, 52 'God damn me;' that's as much as to say, 'God make me a light wench.' It is written, they appear to men like angels of light: light is an effect of fire, and fire will burn; *ergo,* light 56 wenches will burn. Come not near her.

Cour. Your man and you are marvellous merry, sir. Will you go with me? we'll mend our dinner here. 60

Dro. S. Master, if you do, expect spoon-meat, so bespeak a long spoon.

Ant. S. Why, Dromio?

Dro. S. Marry, he must have a long spoon 64 that must eat with the devil.

Ant. S. Avoid then, fiend! what tell'st thou me of supping?
Thou art, as you are all, a sorceress:
I conjure thee to leave me and be gone. 68

Cour. Give me the ring of mine you had at dinner,
Or, for my diamond, the chain you promis'd,
And I'll be gone, sir, and not trouble you.

Dro. S. Some devils ask but the parings of one's nail, 72
A rush, a hair, a drop of blood, a pin,
A nut, a cherry-stone;
But she, more covetous, would have a chain.

47 avoid: *avaunt*   51 light: *wanton*
59, 60 mend our dinner: *i.e. supplement it by further refreshments*

Master, be wise: an if you give it her,   76
The devil will shake her chain and fright us with it.

   Cour. I pray you, sir, my ring, or else the chain:
I hope you do not mean to cheat me so.

   Ant. S. Avaunt, thou witch!   Come, Dromio, let us
     go.   80

   Dro. S. 'Fly pride,' says the peacock: mistress, that
     you know.

              Exit [*Dromio of Syracuse with his master*].

   Cour. Now, out of doubt, Antipholus is mad,
Else would he never so demean himself.
A ring he hath of mine worth forty ducats,   84
And for the same he promis'd me a chain:
Both one and other he denies me now.
The reason that I gather he is mad,
Besides this present instance of his rage,   88
Is a mad tale he told to-day at dinner,
Of his own doors being shut against his entrance.
Belike his wife, acquainted with his fits,
On purpose shut the doors against his way.   92
My way is now to hie home to his house,
And tell his wife, that, being lunatic,
He rush'd into my house, and took perforce
My ring away.   This course I fittest choose,   96
For forty ducats is too much to lose.   [*Exit.*]

Scene Four

[*A Street*]

Enter Antipholus Ephes. with a Gaoler.

   Ant. E. Fear me not, man; I will not break away:
I'll give thee, ere I leave thee, so much money,

81 'Fly . . . peacock: *cf. n.*   83 demean: *conduct*

To warrant thee, as I am 'rested for.
My wife is in a wayward mood to-day,　　　　4
And will not lightly trust the messenger.
That I should be attach'd in Ephesus,
I tell you, 'twill sound harshly in her ears.

Enter Dromio Eph. with a rope's end.

Here comes my man: I think he brings the money.　8
How now, sir! have you that I sent you for?

Dro. E. Here's that, I warrant you, will pay them
all.

Ant. E. But where's the money?

Dro. E. Why, sir, I gave the money for the rope.　12

Ant. E. Five hundred ducats, villain, for a rope?

Dro. E. I'll serve you, sir, five hundred at the rate.

Ant. E. To what end did I bid thee hie thee home?

Dro. E. To a rope's end, sir; and to that end am I
return'd.　　　　　16

Ant. E. And to that end, sir, I will welcome you.

[*Beats him.*]

Off. Good sir, be patient.

Dro. E. Nay, 'tis for me to be patient; I am in adversity.

Off. Good now, hold thy tongue.　　　　20

Dro. E. Nay, rather persuade him to hold his
hands.

Ant. E. Thou whoreson, senseless villain!

Dro. E. I would I were senseless, sir, that I　24
might not feel your blows.

Ant. E. Thou art sensible in nothing but
blows, and so is an ass.

Dro. E. I am an ass indeed; you may prove　28
it by my long ears. I have served him from the
hour of my nativity to this instant, and have

20 Good now: *pray you*　　　　　26 sensible: *sensitive*

nothing at his hands for my service but blows.
When I am cold, he heats me with beating; 32
when I am warm, he cools me with beating:
I am waked with it when I sleep, raised with it
when I sit, driven out of doors with it when I go
from home, welcomed home with it when I 36
return; nay, I bear it on my shoulders, as a
beggar wont her brat; and, I think, when he
hath lamed me, I shall beg with it from door to
door.   40

*Enter Adriana, Luciana, Courtesan, and a School-
master, called Pinch.*

  Ant. E. Come, go along; my wife is coming
yonder.
  Dro. E. Mistress, *respice finem,* respect your
end; or rather, to prophesy like the parrot, 44
'Beware the rope's end.'
  Ant. E. Wilt thou still talk?   *Beats Dro.*
  Cour. How say you now? is not your husband mad?
  Adr. His incivility confirms no less.   48
Good Doctor Pinch, you are a conjurer;
Establish him in his true sense again,
And I will please you what you will demand.
  Luc. Alas, how fiery and how sharp he looks!   52
  Cour. Mark how he trembles in his ecstasy!
  Pinch. Give me your hand and let me feel your pulse.
  Ant. E. There is my hand, and let it feel your ear.
                                          [*Strikes him.*]
  Pinch. I charge thee, Satan, hous'd within this
    man,   56
To yield possession to my holy prayers,
And to thy state of darkness hie thee straight:

38 wont: *is wont to*   44, 45 prophesy . . . end; *cf. n.*
49 conjurer; *cf. n.*   51 please: *pay*   53 ecstasy: *madness*

I conjure thee by all the saints in heaven.

 Ant. E. Peace, doting wizard, peace! I am not
  mad.   60

 Adr. O that thou wert not, poor distressed soul!

 Ant. E. You minion, you, are these your customers?
Did this companion with the saffron face
Revel and feast it at my house to-day,   64
Whilst upon me the guilty doors were shut
And I denied to enter in my house?

 Adr. O husband, God doth know you din'd at home;
Where would you had remain'd until this time,   68
Free from these slanders and this open shame!

 Ant. E. Din'd at home! Thou villain, what say'st
  thou?

 Dro. E. Sir, sooth to say, you did not dine at home.

 Ant. E. Were not my doors lock'd up and I shut
  out?   72

 Dro. E. Perdy, your doors were lock'd and you shut
  out.

 Ant. E. And did not she herself revile me there?

 Dro. E. Sans fable, she herself revil'd you there.

 Ant. E. Did not her kitchen-maid rail, taunt, and
  scorn me?   76

 Dro. E. Certes, she did; the kitchen-vestal scorn'd
  you.

 Ant. E. And did not I in rage depart from thence?

 Dro. E. In verity you did: my bones bear witness,
That since have felt the vigour of his rage.   80

 Adr. Is 't good to soothe him in these contraries?

 Pinch. It is no shame: the fellow finds his vein,
And, yielding to him, humours well his frenzy.

---

62 customers: *guests (used contemptuously)*
73 Perdy: *a corruption of 'par Dieu'*
77 kitchen-vestal; *cf. n.*

75 Sans: *without*
81 soothe: *humor*

Ant. E. Thou hast suborn'd the goldsmith to arrest
    me.   84

Adr. Alas! I sent you money to redeem you,
By Dromio here, who came in haste for it.

Dro. E. Money by me! heart and good will you
    might;
But surely, master, not a rag of money.   88

Ant. E. Went'st not thou to her for a purse of
    ducats?

Adr. He came to me, and I deliver'd it.

Luc. And I am witness with her that she did.

Dro. E. God and the rope-maker bear me witness 92
That I was sent for nothing but a rope!

Pinch. Mistress, both man and master is possess'd:
I know it by their pale and deadly looks.
They must be bound and laid in some dark room.   96

Ant. E. Say, wherefore didst thou lock me forth
    to-day?
And why dost thou deny the bag of gold?

Adr. I did not, gentle husband, lock thee forth.

Dro. E. And, gentle master, I receiv'd no gold;   100
But I confess, sir, that we were lock'd out.

Adr. Dissembling villain! thou speak'st false in both.

Ant. E. Dissembling harlot! thou art false in all,
And art confederate with a damned pack   104
To make a loathsome abject scorn of me;
But with these nails I'll pluck out these false eyes
That would behold in me this shameful sport.

Enter three or four, and offer to bind him. He strives.

Adr. O, bind him, bind him! let him not come near
    me.   108

88 rag: *bit*   95 deadly: *deathly*
96 bound . . . dark room: *old-fashioned treatment of madness*

Pinch. More company! the fiend is strong within
    him.

Luc. Ay me, poor man, how pale and wan he looks!

Ant. E. What, will you murther me? Thou gaoler,
    thou,

I am thy prisoner: wilt thou suffer them   112
To make a rescue?

Off.   Masters, let him go:
He is my prisoner, and you shall not have him.

Pinch. Go bind this man, for he is frantic too.

                 [They bind Dromio of Ephesus.]

Adr. What wilt thou do, thou peevish officer?   116
Hast thou delight to see a wretched man
Do outrage and displeasure to himself?

Off. He is my prisoner: if I let him go,
The debt he owes will be requir'd of me.   120

Adr. I will discharge thee ere I go from thee:
Bear me forthwith unto his creditor,
And, knowing how the debt grows, I will pay it.
Good Master Doctor, see him safe convey'd   124
Home to my house. O most unhappy day!

Ant. E. O most unhappy strumpet!

Dro. E. Master, I am here enter'd in bond for you.

Ant. E. Out on thee, villain! wherefore dost thou
    mad me?   128

Dro. E. Will you be bound for nothing? be
mad, good master: cry, 'the devil!'

Luc. God help, poor souls, how idly do they talk!

Adr. Go bear him hence. Sister, go you with
    me.—   132

Exeunt. Mane[n]*t Offic*[er,] *Adri*[ana,] *Luci*[ana,]
                             Courtesan.

Say now, whose suit is he arrested at?

116 peevish: *foolish*   126 unhappy: *mischievous*

Off. One Angelo, a goldsmith; do you know him?

Adr. I know the man.   What is the sum he owes?

Off. Two hundred ducats.

Adr.   Say, how grows it due? 136

Off. Due for a chain your husband had of him.

Adr. He did bespeak a chain for me, but had it not.

Cour. When as your husband all in rage to-day

Came to my house, and took away my ring—   140

The ring I saw upon his finger now—

Straight after did I meet him with a chain.

Adr. It may be so, but I did never see it.

Come, gaoler, bring me where the goldsmith is: 144

I long to know the truth hereof at large.

Enter Antipholus Siracusia with his Rapier drawn,
and Dromio Sirac.

Luc. God, for thy mercy! they are loose again.

Adr. And come with naked swords.   Let's call more
help

To have them bound again.   *Run all out.*

Off.   Away! they'll kill us. 148

          Exeunt omnes, as fast as may be, frighted.
          [Manent Antipholus and Dromio.]

Ant. S. I see these witches are afraid of swords.

Dro. S. She that would be your wife now ran from
you.

Ant. S. Come to the Centaur; fetch our stuff from
thence:

I long that we were safe and sound aboard.   152

     Dro. S. Faith, stay here this night; they will
surely do us no harm; you saw they speak us
fair, give us gold: methinks they are such a
gentle nation, that, but for the mountain of mad 156

139 When as: *when*   151 stuff: *baggage*

flesh that claims marriage of me, I could find in
my heart to stay here still, and turn witch.

Ant. S. I will not stay to-night for all the town;
Therefore away, to get our stuff aboard.   160

                     Exeunt.

ACT FIFTH

Scene One

[A Street before an Abbey]

Enter the Merchant and [Angelo,] the Goldsmith.

  Ang. I am sorry, sir, that I have hinder'd you;
But, I protest, he had the chain of me,
Though most dishonestly he doth deny it.

  Mer. How is the man esteem'd here in the city?   4

  Ang. Of very reverend reputation, sir,
Of credit infinite, highly belov'd,
Second to none that lives here in the city:
His word might bear my wealth at any time.   8

  Mer. Speak softly: yonder, as I think, he walks.

*Enter Antipholus [of Syracuse] and Dromio [of
Syracuse] again.*

  Ang. 'Tis so; and that self chain about his neck
Which he forswore most monstrously to have.
Good sir, draw near to me, I'll speak to him.   12
Signior Antipholus, I wonder much
That you would put me to this shame and trouble;
And not without some scandal to yourself,
With circumstance and oaths so to deny   16
This chain which now you wear so openly:
Beside the charge, the shame, imprisonment,

8 *Cf. n.*   10 self: *same*   16 circumstance: *particulars*

You have done wrong to this my honest friend,
Who, but for staying on our controversy,   20
Had hoisted sail and put to sea to-day.
This chain you had of me; can you deny it?
    Ant. S. I think I had: I never did deny it.
    Mer. Yes, that you did, sir, and forswore it too.   24
    Ant. S. Who heard me to deny it or forswear it?
    Mer. These ears of mine, thou know'st, did hear thee.
Fie on thee, wretch! 'tis pity that thou liv'st
To walk where any honest men resort.   28
    Ant. S. Thou art a villain to impeach me thus:
I'll prove mine honour and mine honesty
Against thee presently, if thou dar'st stand.
    Mer. I dare, and do defy thee for a villain.   32

*They draw. Enter Adriana, Luciana, Courtesan,
            and others.*

    Adr. Hold! hurt him not, for God's sake! he is mad.
Some get within him, take his sword away.
Bind Dromio too, and bear them to my house.
    Dro. S. Run, master, run; for God's sake, take a
        house!   36
This is some priory: in, or we are spoil'd!
                    *Exeunt [Antipholus of Syracuse and
                        Dromio of Syracuse] to the Priory.*

                    Enter Lady Abbess.

    Abb. Be quiet, people. Wherefore throng you
        hither?
    Adr. To fetch my poor distracted husband hence.
Let us come in, that we may bind him fast,   40
And bear him home for his recovery.
    Ang. I knew he was not in his perfect wits.
    Mer. I am sorry now that I did draw on him.

34 within him: *within his guard*   36 take: *i.e. take refuge in*

Abb. How long hath this possession held the man? 44

Adr. This week he hath been heavy, sour, sad,
And much different from the man he was;
But till this afternoon his passion
Ne'er brake into extremity of rage.   48

Abb. Hath he not lost much wealth by wrack of sea?
Buried some dear friend?   Hath not else his eye
Stray'd his affection in unlawful love—
A sin prevailing much in youthful men,   52
Who give their eyes the liberty of gazing?
Which of these sorrows is he subject to?

Adr. To none of these, except it be the last;
Namely, some love that drew him oft from home.   56

Abb. You should for that have reprehended him.

Adr. Why, so I did.

Abb.   Ay, but not rough enough.

Adr. As roughly as my modesty would let me.

Abb. Haply, in private.

Adr.   And in assemblies too.   60

Abb. Ay, but not enough.

Adr. It was the copy of our conference:
In bed, he slept not for my urging it;
At board, he fed not for my urging it;   64
Alone, it was the subject of my theme;
In company I often glanced it:
Still did I tell him it was vile and bad.

Abb. And thereof came it that the man was mad: 68
The venom clamours of a jealous woman
Poisons more deadly than a mad dog's tooth.
It seems, his sleeps were hinder'd by thy railing,
And thereof comes it that his head is light.   72
Thou say'st his meat was sauc'd with thy upbraidings:
Unquiet meals make ill digestions;

49 wrack of sea: *shipwreck*   51 Stray'd: *led astray*
62 copy: *theme*   66 glanced: *hinted at*

Thereof the raging fire of fever bred:
And what's a fever but a fit of madness?   76
Thou say'st his sports were hinder'd by thy brawls:
Sweet recreation barr'd, what doth ensue
But moody and dull melancholy,
Kinsman to grim and comfortless despair,   80
And at her heels a huge infectious troop
Of pale distemperatures and foes to life?
In food, in sport, and life-preserving rest
To be disturb'd, would mad or man or beast: 84
The consequence is then, thy jealous fits
Hath scar'd thy husband from the use of wits.

  Luc. She never reprehended him but mildly
When he demean'd himself rough, rude, and wildly. 88
Why bear you these rebukes and answer not?

  Adr. She did betray me to my own reproof.
Good people, enter, and lay hold on him.

  Abb. No, not a creature enters in my house.   92

  Adr. Then, let your servants bring my husband
     forth.

  Abb. Neither: he took this place for sanctuary,
And it shall privilege him from your hands
Till I have brought him to his wits again,   96
Or lose my labour in assaying it.

  Adr. I will attend my husband, be his nurse,
Diet his sickness, for it is my office,
And will have no attorney but myself;   100
And therefore let me have him home with me.

  Abb. Be patient; for I will not let him stir
Till I have us'd the approved means I have,
With wholesome syrups, drugs, and holy prayers,   104
To make of him a formal man again.
It is a branch and parcel of mine oath,

---

82 distemperatures: *disorders*   105 formal: *rational*
106 parcel: *part*

A charitable duty of my order;
Therefore depart and leave him here with me. 108
    Adr. I will not hence and leave my husband here;
And ill it doth beseem your holiness
To separate the husband and the wife.
    Abb. Be quiet, and depart: thou shalt not have
        him. [*Exit.*] 112
    Luc. Complain unto the duke of this indignity.
    Adr. Come, go: I will fall prostrate at his feet,
And never rise until my tears and prayers
Have won his Grace to come in person hither, 116
And take perforce my husband from the abbess.
    Sec. Mer. By this, I think, the dial points at five:
Anon, I'm sure, the duke himself in person
Comes this way to the melancholy vale, 120
The place of death and sorry execution,
Behind the ditches of the abbey here.
    Ang. Upon what cause?
    Sec. Mer. To see a reverend Syracusian mer-
        chant, 124
Who put unluckily into this bay
Against the laws and statutes of this town,
Beheaded publicly for his offence.
    Ang. See where they come: we will behold his
        death. 128
    Luc. Kneel to the duke before he pass the abbey.

*Enter the Duke of Ephesus, and [Ægeon] the Mer-
    chant of Syracuse, bare head, with the Heads-
    man, and other Officers.*

    Duke. Yet once again proclaim it publicly,
If any friend will pay the sum for him,
He shall not die; so much we tender him. 132

121 sorry: *sad*
132 so much . . . him: *so much leniency do we offer him*

Adr. Justice, most sacred duke, against the abbess!

Duke. She is a virtuous and a reverend lady:
It cannot be that she hath done thee wrong.

Adr. May it please your Grace, Antipholus, my
    husband,   136
Who I made lord of me and all I had,
At your important letters, this ill day
A most outrageous fit of madness took him,
That desperately he hurried through the street,— 140
With him his bondman, all as mad as he,—
Doing displeasure to the citizens
By rushing in their houses, bearing thence
Rings, jewels, anything his rage did like.   144
Once did I get him bound and sent him home,
Whilst to take order for the wrongs I went
That here and there his fury had committed.
Anon, I wot not by what strong escape,   148
He broke from those that had the guard of him,
And with his mad attendant and himself,
Each one with ireful passion, with drawn swords
Met us again, and, madly bent on us,   152
Chas'd us away, till, raising of more aid,
We came again to bind them.   Then they fled
Into this abbey, whither we pursu'd them;
And here the abbess shuts the gates on us,   156
And will not suffer us to fetch him out,
Nor send him forth that we may bear him hence.
Therefore, most gracious duke, with thy command
Let him be brought forth, and borne hence for help. 160

Duke. Long since thy husband serv'd me in my wars,
And I to thee engag'd a prince's word,
When thou didst make him master of thy bed,

---

137 Who: *whom*   138 important: *importunate, urgent*
146 order for: *measures for settling*

To do him all the grace and good I could.   164
Go, some of you, knock at the abbey gate
And bid the lady abbess come to me.
I will determine this before I stir.

Enter a Messenger.

Mess. O mistress, mistress, shift and save your-
self!   168
My master and his man are both broke loose,
Beaten the maids a-row and bound the doctor,
Whose beard they have sing'd off with brands of fire;
And ever as it blaz'd they threw on him   172
Great pails of puddled mire to quench the hair.
My master preaches patience to him, and the while
His man with scissors nicks him like a fool;
And sure, unless you send some present help,   176
Between them they will kill the conjurer.

Adr. Peace, fool! thy master and his man are here,
And that is false thou dost report to us.

Mess. Mistress, upon my life, I tell you true;   180
I have not breath'd almost, since I did see it.
He cries for you and vows, if he can take you,
To scorch your face, and to disfigure you.

Cry within.

Hark, hark! I hear him, mistress: fly, be gone!   184

Duke. Come, stand by me; fear nothing. Guard with
halberds!

Adr. Ay me, it is my husband! Witness you,
That he is borne about invisible:
Even now we hous'd him in the abbey here,   188
And now he's there, past thought of human reason.

167 S. d. Messenger: *i.e. one of Adriana's servants*
170 Beaten: *have beaten*   a-row: *one after another*
175 nicks . . . fool; *cf. n.*   176 present: *immediate*
183 scorch; *cf. n.*

Enter Antipholus [of Ephesus] and Dromio
of Ephesus.

Ant. E. Justice, most gracious duke! O grant me
    justice,
Even for the service that long since I did thee,
When I bestrid thee in the wars and took   192
Deep scars to save thy life; even for the blood
That then I lost for thee, now grant me justice.

Æge. Unless the fear of death doth make me dote,
I see my son Antipholus and Dromio!   196

Ant. E. Justice, sweet prince, against that woman
    there!
She whom thou gav'st to me to be my wife,
That hath abused and dishonour'd me,
Even in the strength and height of injury!   200
Beyond imagination is the wrong
That she this day hath shameless thrown on me.

Duke. Discover how, and thou shalt find me just.

Ant. E. This day, great duke, she shut the doors
    upon me,   204
While she with harlots feasted in my house.

Duke. A grievous fault! Say, woman, didst thou so?

Adr. No, my good lord: myself, he, and my sister
To-day did dine together. So befall my soul   208
As this is false he burthens me withal!

Luc. Ne'er may I look on day, nor sleep on night,
But she tells to your highness simple truth!

Ang. O perjur'd woman! They are both for-
    sworn: 212
In this the madman justly chargeth them.

Ant. E. My liege, I am advised what I say:
Neither disturbed with the effect of wine,

192 bestrid: *stood over (to defend when fallen)*
205 harlots: *lewd fellows*   209 burthens: *charges*
210 on night: *at night*   214 I . . . say: *I speak with due deliberation*

Nor heady-rash, provok'd with raging ire,   216
Albeit my wrongs might make one wiser mad.
This woman lock'd me out this day from dinner:
That goldsmith there, were he not pack'd with her,
Could witness it, for he was with me then;   220
Who parted with me to go fetch a chain,
Promising to bring it to the Porpentine,
Where Balthazar and I did dine together.
Our dinner done, and he not coming thither,   224
I went to seek him: in the street I met him,
And in his company that gentleman.
There did this perjur'd goldsmith swear me down
That I this day of him receiv'd the chain,   228
Which, God he knows, I saw not; for the which
He did arrest me with an officer.
I did obey, and sent my peasant home
For certain ducats: he with none return'd.   232
Then fairly I bespoke the officer
To go in person with me to my house.
By the way we met
My wife, her sister, and a rabble more   236
Of vile confederates: along with them
They brought one Pinch, a hungry lean-fac'd villain,
A mere anatomy, a mountebank,
A threadbare juggler, and a fortune-teller,   240
A needy, hollow-ey'd, sharp-looking wretch,
A living dead man.   This pernicious slave,
Forsooth, took on him as a conjurer,
And, gazing in mine eyes, feeling my pulse,   244
And with no face, as 'twere, out-facing me,
Cries out, I was possess'd.   Then all together
They fell upon me, bound me, bore me thence,
And in a dark and dankish vault at home   248

219 pack'd: *in league*   231 peasant: *servant*
239 anatomy: *skeleton*

There left me and my man, both bound together;
Till, gnawing with my teeth my bonds in sunder,
I gain'd my freedom, and immediately
Ran hither to your Grace; whom I beseech   252
To give me ample satisfaction
For these deep shames and great indignities.

Ang. My lord, in truth, thus far I witness with him,
That he din'd not at home, but was lock'd out.   256

Duke. But had he such a chain of thee, or no?

Ang. He had, my lord; and when he ran in here,
These people saw the chain about his neck.

Sec. Mer. Besides, I will be sworn these ears of
    mine   260
Heard you confess you had the chain of him,
After you first forswore it on the mart;
And thereupon I drew my sword on you;
And then you fled into this abbey here,   264
From whence, I think, you are come by miracle.

Ant. E. I never came within these abbey walls;
Nor ever didst thou draw thy sword on me;
I never saw the chain, so help me heaven!   268
And this is false you burthen me withal.

Duke. Why, what an intricate impeach is this!
I think you all have drunk of Circe's cup.
If here you hous'd him, here he would have been;   272
If he were mad, he would not plead so coldly;
You say he din'd at home; the goldsmith here
Denies that saying. Sirrah, what say you?

Dro. E. Sir, he din'd with her there, at the Por-
    pentine.   276

Cour. He did, and from my finger snatch'd that ring.

Ant. E. 'Tis true, my liege; this ring I had of her.

Duke. Saw'st thou him enter at the abbey here?

270 impeach: *accusation*   271 Circe's cup; *cf. n.*
273 coldly: *coolly*

 Cour. As sure, my liege, as I do see your Grace. 280

 Duke. Why, this is strange. Go call the abbess
  hither.

I think you are all mated or stark mad.

Exit one to the Abbess.

 Æge. Most mighty duke, vouchsafe me speak a word:

Haply I see a friend will save my life, 284

And pay the sum that may deliver me.

 Duke. Speak freely, Syracusian, what thou wilt.

 Æge. Is not your name, sir, called Antipholus?

And is not that your bondman Dromio? 288

 Dro. E. Within this hour I was his bondman, sir;

But he, I thank him, gnaw'd in two my cords:

Now am I Dromio and his man, unbound.

 Æge. I am sure you both of you remember me. 292

 Dro. E. Ourselves we do remember, sir, by you;

For lately we were bound, as you are now.

You are not Pinch's patient, are you, sir?

 Æge. Why look you strange on me? you know me
  well. 296

 Ant. E. I never saw you in my life till now.

 Æge. O, grief hath chang'd me since you saw me last,

And careful hours, with Time's deformed hand,

Have written strange defeatures in my face: 300

But tell me yet, dost thou not know my voice?

 Ant. E. Neither.

 Æge. Dromio, nor thou?

 Dro. E. No, trust me, sir, not I. 304

 Æge. I am sure thou dost.

 Dro. E. Ay, sir; but I am sure I do not; and

whatsoever a man denies, you are now bound

to believe him. 308

 Æge. Not know my voice! O time's extremity,

299 careful: *full of care* deformed: *deforming*

Hast thou so crack'd and splitted my poor tongue
In seven short years, that here my only son
Knows not my feeble key of untun'd cares?　　　312
Though now this grained face of mine be hid
In sap-consuming winter's drizzled snow,
And all the conduits of my blood froze up,
Yet hath my night of life some memory,　　　316
My wasting lamps some fading glimmer left,
My dull deaf ears a little use to hear:
All these old witnesses—I cannot err—
Tell me thou art my son Antipholus.　　　320

　　Ant. E. I never saw my father in my life.

　　Æge. But seven years since, in Syracusa, boy,
Thou know'st we parted: but perhaps, my son,
Thou sham'st to acknowledge me in misery.　　　324

　　Ant. E. The duke and all that know me in the city
Can witness with me that it is not so:
I ne'er saw Syracusa in my life.

　　Duke. I tell thee, Syracusian, twenty years　　　328
Have I been patron to Antipholus,
During which time he ne'er saw Syracusa.
I see thy age and dangers make thee dote.

Enter the Abbess, with Antipholus Siracusa and
Dromio Sir.

　　Abb. Most mighty duke, behold a man much
　　　wrong'd.　　　　　　*All gather to see them.* 332
　　Adr. I see two husbands, or mine eyes deceive me!
　　Duke. One of these men is Genius to the other;
And so of these, which is the natural man,
And which the spirit? Who deciphers them?　　　336
　　Dro. S. I, sir, am Dromio: command him away.
　　Dro. E. I, sir, am Dromio: pray let me stay.

312 my . . . cares; *cf. n.*　　　　313 grained: *furrowed*
334 Genius: *attendant spirit*　　　336 deciphers: *distinguishes*

Ant. S. Ægeon art thou not? or else his ghost?

Dro. S. O, my old master! who hath bound him
    here?   340

Abb. Whoever bound him, I will loose his bonds,
And gain a husband by his liberty.
Speak, old Ægeon, if thou be'st the man
That hadst a wife once call'd Æmilia,   344
That bore thee at a burthen two fair sons.
O, if thou be'st the same Ægeon, speak,
And speak unto the same Æmilia!

Æge. If I dream not, thou art Æmilia: 348
If thou art she, tell me where is that son
That floated with thee on the fatal raft?

Abb. By men of Epidamnum, he and I
And the twin Dromio, all were taken up;   352
But by and by rude fishermen of Corinth
By force took Dromio and my son from them,
And me they left with those of Epidamnum.
What then became of them, I cannot tell;   356
I to this fortune that you see me in.

Duke. Why, here begins his morning story right:
These two Antipholus', these two so like,
And these two Dromios, one in semblance,—   360
Besides her urging of her wreck at sea,—
These are the parents to these children,
Which accidentally are met together.
Antipholus, thou cam'st from Corinth first?   364

Ant. S. No, sir, not I; I came from Syracuse.

Duke. Stay, stand apart; I know not which is which.

Ant. E. I came from Corinth, my most gracious
    lord,—

Dro. E. And I with him.   368

358-363 *Cf. n.*

 Ant. E. Brought to this town by that most famous
  warrior,
Duke Menaphon, your most renowned uncle.
 Adr. Which of you two did dine with me to-day?
 Ant. S. I, gentle mistress.   372
 Adr. And are not you my husband?
 Ant. E. No; I say nay to that.
 Ant. S. And so do I; yet did she call me so;
And this fair gentlewoman, her sister here, 376
Did call me brother. [*To Luciana.*] What I told you
  then,
I hope I shall have leisure to make good,
If this be not a dream I see and hear.
 Ang. That is the chain, sir, which you had of me. 380
 Ant. S. I think it be, sir; I deny it not.
 Ant. E. And you, sir, for this chain arrested me.
 Ang. I think I did, sir; I deny it not.
 Adr. I sent you money, sir, to be your bail, 384
By Dromio; but I think he brought it not.
 Dro. E. No, none by me.
 Ant. S. This purse of ducats I receiv'd from you,
And Dromio, my man, did bring them me. 388
I see we still did meet each other's man,
And I was ta'en for him, and he for me;
And thereupon these errors are arose.
 Ant. E. These ducats pawn I for my father here. 392
 Duke. It shall not need: thy father hath his life.
 Cour. Sir, I must have that diamond from you.
 Ant. E. There, take it; and much thanks for my
  good cheer.
 Abb. Renowned duke, vouchsafe to take the pains 396
To go with us into the abbey here,
And hear at large discoursed all our fortunes;

389 still: *continually*

And all that are assembled in this place,
That by this sympathized one day's error   400
Have suffer'd wrong, go keep us company,
And we shall make full satisfaction.
Thirty-three years have I but gone in travail
Of you, my sons; and, till this present hour   404
My heavy burthen ne'er delivered.
The duke, my husband, and my children both,
And you the calendars of their nativity,
Go to a gossip's feast, and go with me: 408
After so long grief such festivity!

>   *Duke.* With all my heart I'll gossip at this feast.
>>   *Exeunt omnes. Mane[n]t the two Dromios
>>   and two Brothers.*

>   *Dro. S.* Master, shall I fetch your stuff from ship-
>   board?

>   *Ant. E.* Dromio, what stuff of mine hast thou em-
>   bark'd?   412

>   *Dro. S.* Your goods that lay at host, sir, in the
>   Centaur.

>   *Ant. S.* He speaks to me. I am your master, Dromio:
Come, go with us; we'll look to that anon:
Embrace thy brother there; rejoice with him.   416
>>   *Exit [with his Brother].*

>   *Dro. S.* There is a fat friend at your master's house,
That kitchen'd me for you to-day at dinner:
She now shall be my sister, not my wife.

>   *Dro. E.* Methinks you are my glass, and not my
>   brother: 420
I see by you I am a sweet-fac'd youth.
Will you walk in to see their gossiping?

400 sympathized: *shared by all*   403 Thirty-three years; *cf. n.*
407 calendars . . . nativity; *cf. n.*
408 gossip's: *baptismal sponsor's*   410 gossip: *make merry*
413 lay at host: *were put up*
418 kitchen'd: *entertained* (*in the kitchen*)

Dro. S. Not I, sir; you are my elder.

Dro. E. That's a question: how shall we try it? 424

Dro. S. We'll draw cuts for the senior: till then lead
thou first.

Dro. E. Nay, then, thus:

We came into the world like brother and brother;

And now let's go hand in hand, not one before another.

Exeunt.

425 cuts: *lots*

FINIS.

NOTES

I. i. 8. *guilders.* The word is anachronistically used here, and in IV. i. 4, in a general sense for 'money,' without particular reference to the Dutch coin.

I. i. 11. *intestine.* This word occurs in *1 Henry IV*, I. i. 12, where it means 'internal, civil,' and refers to wars within the state. Though it can hardly have that precise meaning here, it seems to carry a similar implication of a violent disturbance of the peace between people who ought to dwell in amity with one another. By his use of the word 'seditious,' in the next line, Solinus implies that the strife between Syracuse and Ephesus has been in the nature of a civil war.

I. i. 34. *nature.* Ægeon wishes it to be remembered, after his death, that it was not the commission of a crime which brought him to his end, but the natural affection which led him to Ephesus, in quest of his son.

I. i. 41. *Epidamnum.* 'Epidamium' in the Folio. The correct name of the town is Epidamnus (afterwards called by the Romans 'Dyrrhachium'). It is the modern Durazzo in Albania, on the Adriatic. The fact that the accusative form 'Epidamnum' is used in the translation of the *Menæchmi* published in 1595 has been taken as evidence that Shakespeare saw that translation in manuscript before he wrote *The Comedy of Errors.* Cf. Appendix A.

I. i. 78. *latter-born.* From line 124, we learn that it was the younger of the twins who was rescued with his father; and some editors, forgetting that Ægeon is describing the confusion of a shipwreck, have emended the text to correct the apparent inconsistency.

I. i. 93. *Epidaurus.* 'Epidarus' in the Folio. A town in Argolis, on the Saronic Gulf. Corinth had a port situated on the same gulf.

I. i. 151. *life.* Craig accepts this emendation, proposed by Rowe, for 'helpe' in the Folio; but *health*, which has been adopted by some other editors, seems equally satisfactory.

I. ii. S. d. *Enter Antipholus Erotes.* 'Erotes' is probably a corruption of 'Erraticus,' i.e. the Wanderer. Compare the note on II. i. S. d. below.

I. ii. 41. *almanac of my true date.* Because both master and man were born in the same hour, Antipholus can refer to his slave as the almanac by which he can discover the date of his birth.

I. ii. 63. *post.* Dromio plays upon two meanings of the word. In the next line, he refers to the post, in a tavern or shop, upon which accounts were 'scored' with chalk or notches.

I. ii. 75. *Phœnix.* Probably the sign over the shop of Antipholus of Ephesus, who is a merchant; but private houses, as well as inns and shops, were sometimes distinguished by names that had reference to some distinctive carving or other decoration.

II. i. S. d. *wife to Antipholus Sereptus.* The distinguishing epithet 'Sereptus' is an apparent error for 'Surreptus,' the Lost or Stolen. In the *Menæchmi* of Plautus, one of the twins was stolen from his parents and the other wandered about in search of him. Compare the note on I. ii. S. d. above. The possible relation of these corrupt Latin epithets to a lost source of the play is discussed in Appendix A.

II. i. 15. *lash'd.* Perhaps there is a play upon another meaning of the word; viz. 'bound, fastened.'

II. i. 57. *horn-mad.* Merely, 'mad as a horned beast,' i.e. a bull or buck; but Adriana is probably right in suspecting a reference to the ancient jest to the effect that the cuckold wore invisible horns.

II. i. 82. *round.* Dromio plays upon two meanings of the word: (1) spherical, (2) plain-spoken.

II. i. 109-113. *I see, the jewel best enamelled Will*

lose his beauty; yet the gold bides still That others
touch, and often touching will Wear gold; and no man
that hath a name, By falsehood and corruption doth it
shame. 'The best enamelled jewel tarnishes; but the
gold setting keeps its lustre however it may be worn
by the touch; similarly, a man of assured reputation,
can commit domestic infidelity without blasting it.'
(Herford.) This interpretation of the passage seems
quite as satisfactory as those offered by editors who
have emended the reading of the Folio more exten-
sively. Theobald's suggestion of *wear,* for the Folio
where, appears to be the only necessary emendation.
At best, the meaning is obscure, and it may be a correct conjecture that some lines have dropped out of
the text, which is obviously corrupt.

II. ii. 24. *earnest.* Used with quibbling reference
to 'earnest money,' i.e. money paid to bind a bargain.

II. ii. 29. *And make a common of my serious hours.*
'That is, intrude on them when you please. The allusion is to those tracts of ground destined to common
use, which are thence called commons' (Steevens).

II. ii. 32. *aspect.* Probably there is an allusion to
the astrological use of the word to denote the favorable
or unfavorable influences of the planets.

II. ii. 37. *sconce.* The dialogue contains a play on
three meanings of the word. Antipholus uses it in the
slang sense of 'head'; and Dromio, when he speaks of
'battering,' refers to the meaning, 'a small fort,' to
which he returns when he uses the word 'insconce' in
line 38. In this line it obviously means some form of
head-armor.

II. ii. 64. *choleric.* Overdone meat was supposed
to induce irascibility. Compare *The Taming of the
Shrew,* IV. i. 173-175:

'I tell thee, Kate, 'twas burnt and dried away;
　And I expressly am forbid to touch it,
　For it engenders choler, planteth anger.'

II. ii. 76. *fine and recovery.* A legal process by which entailed estates might be transferred from one owner to another.

II. ii. 87, 88. *he hath the wit to lose his hair.* In this expression, which seems to have been in the nature of a proverb, Dr. Johnson suspects a reference to the loss of hair through diseases contracted in licentiousness.

II. ii. 92. *jollity.* The word hardly seems to fit the context, and some editors read 'policy,' following a conjecture by Staunton.

II. ii. 101. *tiring.* The Folio reads 'trying'; corrected by Pope. A tire was a headdress or wig.

II. ii. 150. *distain'd.* The word is used elsewhere by Shakespeare with the meaning given in the gloss. The emendation 'unstain'd,' accepted by Craig, appears, at first sight, to fit the context better; but the line as it stands may be taken as a climax to Adriana's outburst against the injustice of the so-called 'double standard,' a matter to which she seems to refer in the obscure passage at II. i. 109-113. There seems to be no necessity for following the most recent Cambridge editors in transposing lines 149 and 150.

II. ii. 209. *laughs.* The common (Northern English) verbal plural in —s. Compare 'poisons,' V. i. 70.

III. i. 46, 47. *If thou hadst been Dromio to-day in my place, Thou wouldst have chang'd thy face for a name, or thy name for an ass.* If you had been in my place to-day, you would have been glad to wear some other man's face (and so, under his name, pass unrecognized by Antipholus); for otherwise, you would have endured such a beating as to convince you that you were an ass rather than Dromio. Compare lines 15, 16 above.

III. i. 48. S. d. *Luce.* [*Within.*] The stage direction of the Folio, at this point, reads *Enter Luce;* and below, at line 61, *Enter Adriana.* Dyce was probably right in his suggestion that 'both maid and mistress made their appearance on the balcony termed the upper stage, though they undoubtedly were supposed not to see the persons at the door.'

III. i. 52. *when? can you tell?* A convenient rejoinder, by which an importunate request or query might be turned aside. Compare *1 Henry IV, II.* i. 43.

III. i. 105. *For slander lives upon succession.* That is, slander lives on, in possession of a man's reputation, after his death.

III. ii. S. d. *Luciana.* Erroneously called 'Iuliana' in the Folio, which similarly assigns her first speech to 'Iulia.' The others are correctly marked 'Luc.'

III. ii. 11. *become disloyalty.* Make even your disloyalty appear becoming by assuming an affectionate attitude toward your wife.

III. ii. 52. *Let Love, being light, be drowned if she sink.* Antipholus believes that love is in no danger of being destroyed: it is too buoyant to be drowned. Compare *Venus and Adonis,* 149, 150:

> 'Love is a spirit all compact of fire,
>   Not gross to sink, but light, and will aspire.'

III. ii. 64. *My sole earth's heaven, and my heaven's claim.* 'All the happiness that I wish on earth, and all that I claim from heaven hereafter' (Malone).

III. ii. 93. *'Sir-reverence.'* A contraction of 'save your reverence,' a phrase used by way of apology for a remark that might give offence.

III. ii. 127, 128. *armed and reverted, making war against her heir.* There is undoubtedly a quibbling allusion here to the armed resistance of the Holy League to Henry of Navarre, designated heir to the French throne by Henry III in 1589, and finally crowned King of France, as Henry IV, at Chartres, February, 1594. 'Mistress Nell's brazen forehead seemed to push back her rough and rebellious hair, as France resisted the claim of the Protestant heir to the throne' (Clarke). English interest in the civil war in France had been quickened by the fact that, in 1591, Elizabeth sent an expedition under Sir John Norris and the Earl of Essex to aid Henry in the siege of Rouen.

III. ii. 152. *turn i' the wheel.* 'There is comprehended, under the Curres of the coursest kinde, a certaine dog in kitchen-service excellent. For when any meat is to be roasted, they go into a wheel, which they turning round about with the waight of their bodies, so dilligently looke to their businesse, that no drudge nor scullion can do the feate more cunningly. Whom the popular sort hereupon call Turnespets.' (Topsell: *Historie of Foure-Footed Beastes,* 1607.)

IV. i. 21. *I buy a thousand pound a year.* The point of Dromio's remark is obscure, but he seems to mean that in buying a rope he is purchasing an annuity likely to yield him an income of a thousand beatings (poundings) a year.

IV. i. 56. *send me by some token.* Send me with some sign to attest my right to receive payment for the chain.

IV. i. 94. *sheep.* Shakespeare frequently puns upon this word, which was pronounced short, almost like *ship.*

IV. i. 111. *Dowsabel.* Her name is Nell (cf. III. ii. 112 above); but Dromio ironically applies to her the poetic name, derived from *douce et belle,* frequently used by the Elizabethans to designate a fair lass. Compare Drayton's semi-humorous *Ballad of Dowsabell* (1593).

IV. ii. 6. *his heart's meteors tilting in his face.* Warburton finds here an allusion to the aurora borealis, which, as he remarks, sometimes has 'the appearance of lines of armies meeting in the shock.'

IV. ii. 27. *Far from her nest the lapwing cries away.* That is, to divert attention from the nest and the young birds. This instinctive habit of the lapwing is frequently referred to in Elizabethan literature.

IV. ii. 35. *fairy.* Some editors alter the word, to read *fury,* but emendation is unnecessary. Dromio has in mind the baleful and malevolent disposition sometimes attributed to fairies.

IV. ii. 37. *A back-friend, a shoulder-clapper.* The sergeant usually approached from the rear and arrested his man by laying his hand roughly on the shoulder. *Back-friend* has also the meaning of false friend.

IV. ii. 39. *runs counter.* A hunting term, meaning to follow the scent in the direction opposite to that which the game has taken. The word *counter* was also used of the two Compters, or debtors' prisons, in London, and officers who made arrests for debt were known as 'sergeants of the counter.'

IV. ii. 40. *One that, before the judgment, carries poor souls to hell.* Before the passage of the Debtors' Act of 1869, arrests in civil cases could be made, by what was called 'mesne process,' before final judgment was given. The quibbling reference to the Last Judgment is obvious. 'Hell' was a name given to a prison for confinement of debtors, a sponging house, such as those in Wood street and the Poultry.

IV. ii. 42. *on the case.* 'Dromio S. here appears to quibble on the distinction between "matter" and "case" as a distinction between "contents" and "form." No doubt there is a further reference to the well-known "action on the case," which was a general action for the relief of a civil wrong not especially provided for' (Arden ed.).

IV. ii. 58. *owes more than he's worth to season.* Dromio plays upon the familiar expression 'time and season,' where 'season' means 'favorable opportunity.' Time never furnishes so many opportunities as he ought. The thought is the direct opposite of that expressed in *Macbeth,* I. iii. 147: 'Time and the hour runs through the roughest day.'

IV. iii. 11. *Lapland sorcerers.* Down to the days of Milton, who refers to 'Lapland witches' in *Paradise Lost,* ii. 665, Lapland was frequently mentioned in English literature as the especial home or rendezvous of witches and sorcerers.

IV. iii. 13. *What, have you got the picture of old Adam new apparelled?* Dromio is naturally amazed to discover that his master appears to have shaken off the sergeant, whom he calls *the picture of old Adam* because he was 'in buff,' an expression used colloquially of the bare skin. *New apparelled* cannot be so easily explained, but the idea may be, 'Have you got the sergeant a new *suit?*'

IV. iii. 17, 18. *calf's skin that was killed for the Prodigal.* St. Luke's Gospel, 15. 23.

IV. iii. 81. *'Fly pride,' says the peacock.* An accusation of dishonesty coming from this woman, whom Dromio takes to be dishonest, seems to him as out of place as the warning against pride proverbially attributed to the peacock.

IV. iv. 44, 45. *prophesy like the parrot, 'Beware the rope's end.'* Parrots were frequently taught to use such ill-omened phrases as this, in order to raise a laugh against the person for whom the bird appeared to prophesy an evil fate. There is probably a quibble in the expression *Beware the rope's end,* which is a free translation of *respice funem,* frequently used punningly with *respice finem.*

IV. iv. 49. *conjurer.* As a schoolmaster, Dr. Pinch was in a position to deal with evil spirits in Latin, the only language which they were popularly supposed to understand. Compare *Hamlet,* I. i. 42: 'Thou art a scholar; speak to it, Horatio.'

IV. iv. 77. *kitchen-vestal.* 'Her charge being, like that of the vestal virgins, to keep the fire burning' (Johnson).

V. i. 8. *His word might bear my wealth at any time.* I should always have been ready to trust him for all I was worth.

V. i. 175. *nicks him like a fool.* Court jesters frequently wore their hair trimmed unevenly to give them a ludicrous appearance.

V. i. 183. *scorch.* The reading of the Folio. Some editors believe the word is a misprint for *scotch,* to hack or cut.

V. i. 271. *Circe's cup.* A draught from Circe's cup transformed men into beasts. The Duke means that some such enchantment appears to have fallen on his subjects, rendering them as irrational as animals.

V. i. 312. *my feeble key of untun'd cares.* 'The weak and discordant tone of my voice, that is changed by grief' (Douce).

V. i. 358-363. In the Folio, these lines follow line 347. The rearrangement, first suggested by Capell, has been adopted by most modern editors.

V. i. 403. *Thirty-three years.* This figure is hardly consistent with two of Ægeon's statements; viz. that his eldest son was eighteen when they separated (I. i. 125); and that seven years have since elapsed (V. i. 322); but Shakespeare was frequently careless in such matters.

V. i. 407. *calendars of their nativity.* I.e. the two Dromios. Compare the note on I. ii. 41.

APPENDIX A

SOURCES OF THE PLAY

The plot of *The Comedy of Errors* was derived, directly or indirectly, from the *Menæchmi* of Plautus. Some scholars, mindful of Shakespeare's 'small Latin,' are inclined to believe that his education in the classics had not gone far enough to enable him to read Plautus in the original; and it has been suggested that he may have used an English prose translation, prepared by a certain 'W. W.' This translation, to be sure, was not published until 1595, some years later than the date usually assigned to Shakespeare's play; but the printer, in his note to the reader, hints that the work had existed in manuscript for some time. There is a possibility that Shakespeare had seen it before he wrote his *Errors*. Some verbal resemblances between his play and 'W. W.'s' translation have been pointed out, but they are too slight and too infrequent to be taken as proof that this work was a direct source of *The Comedy of Errors*. It is just as probable that Shakespeare went directly to the Latin text for his material.

The general resemblance between *The Comedy of Errors* and the *Menæchmi* may be indicated by reproducing the argument of the Latin play, which appears in the 1595 translation as follows:

Two Twinborne sonnes, a Sicill marchant had,
Menechmus one, and Sosicles the other:
The first his Father lost a little Lad,
The Grandsire namde the latter like his brother.
This (growne a man) long travell tooke to seeke
His Brother, and to Epidamnum came,
Where th' other dwelt inricht, and him so like,
That Citizens there take him for the same:

> Father, wife, neighbours, each mistaking either,
> Much pleasant Error, ere they meete togither.

Examination of the two plays shows that the similarity extends to the details of the action. Menæchmus the Citizen, in the Latin play, promises to dine with Erotium, a courtesan; but the dinner goes to Menæchmus the Traveller, who has just landed, accompanied by his slave, Messenio, and is mistaken for his brother by the courtesan and her servants. Erotium gives her guest a cloak to take to the dyers and a chain to be repaired by a goldsmith; and Menæchmus the Citizen is later called to account for these articles, which he has not seen since he stole them from his wife and bestowed them on Erotium. Menæchmus the Traveller, encountering his brother's wife, who mistakes him for her husband, is completely at a loss to understand her reproaches. As a result of their behavior in these bewildering circumstances, both brothers are separately suspected of madness, and Medicus, a physician, essays his powers as a conjurer to reduce the malady. Certainly there are scenes in *The Comedy of Errors* which bear a resemblance to these incidents and situations, and they seem to point toward a familiarity, on Shakespeare's part, with the details of Plautus' play, as well as with its general outline.

Shakespeare's treatment of this source material shows characteristic independence. Of the nine persons of the Plautine comedy, he has retained but six: the Menæchmi (Antipholi), Messenio (Dromio of Syracuse), Mulier (Adriana), Erotium (the Courtesan), and Medicus (Dr. Pinch). Such stock characters as the Cook and the Parasite have been discarded, while Luciana has been substituted for Senex, the doddering father-in-law of Menæchmus the Citizen. Dromio of Ephesus, Solinus, Ægeon, Æmilia, Luce, and the Merchants have been added. Similar incidents and situations are given very different treatment by the two poets. The relations between Adriana and her husband are treated less cynically by Shakespeare than in the Latin play, and the dinner with the courtesan is made to appear the natural result of the injured feelings of a man who finds himself unaccountably locked out of his own house: we certainly hear nothing, in *The Comedy of Errors,* of jewelry or a cloak stolen from Adriana and bestowed upon the courtesan. Antipholus of Syracuse, moreover, is less ready to profit by valuable tokens, forced upon him by people obviously laboring under some strange misapprehension, than his prototype, Menæchmus the Traveller, who not only proposes to make off with the courtesan's cloak and chain, but endeavors to wheedle more booty out of her maid.

Of more importance than these differences in treatment are certain significant additions to the rather simple plot, which appear in *The Comedy of Errors,* broadening the humor and making the comedy a richer play than the *Menæchmi.* In Plautus, only one of the twin heroes is attended by his slave, and there is no suggestion of the delightful absurdity of a second pair of identical twins, attendant upon the first. The presence of the two Dromios has enabled Shakespeare to begin the merry game of confusion earlier in the play and to continue it to the end with unfailing variety in the complications. The substitution of Luciana for Senex not only replaces a stock character with a very real and appealing person, but also provides an opportunity for an added sentimental interest and for some love-making in rhymed verse, which anticipates the poetry of *Romeo and Juliet.* Another important addition is the introduction of Ægeon and Æmilia, which places the boisterous farce in a graceful setting of romantic comedy. This embellishment of the plot has every appearance of being Shakespeare's invention, though possible sources have been pointed out in Ariosto's *Suppositi* and in the old and

famous story of Apollonius of Tyre. The scene in
which Antipholus of Ephesus knocks vainly at his
own door, while his brother is entertained within, does
not appear in the *Menæchmi* but resembles a scene in
the *Amphitruo,* another comedy by Plautus.

All these important differences between *The Comedy
of Errors* and its remote Latin original may, of course,
be the fruits of Shakespeare's own labors over his
source material; but a plausible case has been made out
for the existence of an intermediary step in the evolu-
tion of the plot. It has been conjectured that the
comedy is the rewriting of an old play, which had become the property of Shakespeare's company. Support has been found for this theory in the use of the
doggerel fourteen-syllable line in some of the dialogue,
since this form of verse is employed in the surviving
examples of mid-sixteenth century academic comedy.
Another bit of evidence, pointing in the same direction, has been found in the corrupt Latin epithets bestowed upon the twin heroes in some of the stage directions of the Folio. It has been suggested that these
epithets, which are reproduced in the notes,[1] may have
found their way into Shakespeare's play from a gar-
bled transcript of the old comedy which he was rewriting. From the fact that doggerel is used for so
much of the dialogue in the first scene of the third
act, and from the presence, in that scene alone, of the
'ghost' Balthazar and of Luce, who appears to be the
'kitchen-vestal,' elsewhere named Nell, Mr. J. Dover
Wilson argues that we have in a certain part of that
scene a portion of the old play, taken over by Shakespeare practically without revision.

This 'lost source' of Shakespeare's play has been
identified, by those who argue for its existence, with a
performance styled *The Historie of Error,* which was
'shown at Hampton Court on New Yere's daie at night

[1] See notes on I. ii. S. d. and II. i. S. d.

[1576-7], enacted by the children of Powles.' Since the productions given by the boys of St. Paul's were usually derived from classic sources, it seems a plausible conjecture that this lost play was founded upon the *Menæchmi*. The play was given again at Windsor in 1583, if we may believe that the *History of Ferrar* (sic), referred to in the Accounts of the Revels at Court, was the same work.

In the absence of tangible evidence, however, it cannot be definitely stated, either that this lost play was founded upon Plautus, or that it found its way eventually into Shakespeare's hands and formed the basis of his *Comedy of Errors*. Although the theory has gained acceptance, it should be remembered that it rests largely on conjecture and that it begins by assuming the existence of lost evidence which it needs for its support. When all has been said, the fact remains that no principal source for Shakespeare's play, other than the Latin text of the *Menæchmi,* has yet been brought to light.

APPENDIX B

The History of the Play

In 1594, 'betwixt All-hollontide and Christmas,' the gentlemen of Gray's Inn devised revels to grace the coming holiday season, electing one of their number to preside over their festivities as 'Prince of Purpoole.' An account of their revels, obviously written by some choice spirit who had shared in the proceedings and relished their flavor to the full, found its way into print, nearly a century later, in a tract printed for 'W. Canning, at his Shop in the Temple Cloysters MDC-LXXXVIII.' under the title *Gesta Grayorum: or the History of the High and Mighty Prince, Henry Prince of Purpoole . . . Who Reigned and Died A.D. 1594.* This out-of-the-way little volume is valuable for more reasons than one, but its interest for Shakespearians lies in the account which it gives of what happened at Gray's Inn on the night of Holy Innocents (December 28). On that evening, the spirit of revelry seems to have reached its height. An 'ambassador' from the Inner Temple, 'attended by a great number of brave Gentlemen,' put in an appearance about nine of the clock, and it appears that special entertainment of some sort had been devised for their pleasure; but unfortunately 'there arose such a disordered Tumult and Crowd upon the Stage, that there was no opportunity to effect that which was intended.' Indeed, the disorders ran to such length that at last the Lord Ambassador and his train, thinking they were not being 'so kindly entertained as was before expected,' withdrew in some displeasure. 'After their Departure,' the account goes on to record, 'the Throngs and Tumults did somewhat cease, although so much of them continued, as was able to disorder and confound any good Invention whatsoever. In regard whereof, as also for that the Sports intended were especially for the gracing the *Templarians* it was thought good not to offer any thing of Account, saving Dancing and Revelling with Gentlewomen; and after such Sports, a Comedy of Errors (like to *Plautus* his *Menechmus*) was played by the Players. So that Night was begun, and continued to the End, in nothing but Confusion and Errors; whereupon it was ever afterwards called, *The Night of Errors.*'

The players referred to in the account of this night of confusion and errors undoubtedly were the Lord Chamberlain's men (Shakespeare's company), and the play thrust so inauspiciously upon this tumultuous stage, where the confusion was so great as to 'disorder and confound any good Invention whatsoever,' must have been Shakespeare's *Comedy of Errors.* This is the earliest recorded production of the play, but there is no reason to believe that it was a first performance. Indeed, there is evidence indicating that the comedy had been played before the Queen that very afternoon. Payment to the Lord Chamberlain's men was made for a performance at the Court, then at Greenwich, on December 28, and it is a reasonable assumption that the company put on the same bill which they were later to present before the lawyers at Gray's Inn. It should be added that the evening performance was probably not a makeshift, as one might infer from the account in the *Gesta Grayorum.* Undoubtedly, the Prince of Purpoole and his councillors had devised some amateur theatricals of their own for the amusement of their guests from the Inner Temple and found themselves obliged to cancel that part of the entertainment when the spirit of revelry passed beyond their control, in the giddy hours of the early evening; but it seems unlikely that they then called in the players to step into the breach. It is more reasonable to assume, with Sir A. Quiller-Couch, that the performance by the professional company had been prearranged, and that 'the players had been preëmpted from Greenwich to present just such an extravaganza upon Plautus as would tickle the scholarly taste and amuse the "studious lawyers" amid their bowers.'

It is generally agreed that the *Comedy of Errors* was not a new play when it was performed at Gray's Inn in 1594. Every test of versification and language places the comedy among Shakespeare's earliest works; and in the list of his plays given by Francis Meres in the *Palladis Tamia* (1598), 'his *Errors*' stands second, between *The Two Gentlemen of Verona* and *Love's Labour's Lost*. A bit of evidence pointing to a date about 1591 has been found in the text of the play. Dromio of Syracuse, finding out countries in the ample person of Nell, the kitchen-wench, discovers France 'in her forehead, armed and reverted, making war against her heir.' This is usually supposed to be a reference to the armed resistance of the Catholic League against Henry of Navarre, named heir to the throne by Henry III in 1589. Such an allusion would have fallen rather flat after the coronation of Navarre in 1593, but would certainly have taken effect in 1591, when English troops were in France, supporting the cause of the Protestant king against his revolted subjects. This historical allusion, together with a reference, a few lines farther on, to 'whole armadoes of carracks' in connection with Spain, has been taken as evidence to support the date 1591-2, now generally assigned to the play.

The stage history of the comedy, begun amid the tumult of the stormy night at Gray's Inn, has not been conspicuously prosperous. From the Revels Accounts, we learn that '*The Plaie of Errors*, by Shaxberd,' was acted before King James at Whitehall on December 28, 1604. No subsequent performance of the play has been recorded until 1741, when it was revived at Drury Lane. Opening on November 11, the comedy was acted on four successive nights and was put on again on December 10. No bill of the actors in this revival has been preserved, but it is said that Charles Macklin played the part of Dromio of Syracuse.

At Covent Garden, the comedy was revived several times during the eighteenth century. As early as 1734, a comedy in two acts 'taken from Plautus and Shakespeare,' called *See if You Like It, or 'Tis all a Mistake,* was performed there, but we do not know just what relation this play bore to *The Comedy of Errors.* Shakespeare's play was not presented at Covent Garden until April 14, 1762, when it was acted but once. On January 22, 1779, a revised version was performed at the same theatre, probably with the alterations of Thomas Hull, actor, writer, and general utility man of the company. During the next year a farce by W. Woods, called *The Twins, or Which is Which?,* 'altered from Shakespeare's Comedy of Errors,' was produced at the Theatre Royal in Edinburgh; and in April, 1790, a three-act version of Shakespeare's play was performed at Covent Garden. Hull's version came back into its own when it was used as the basis of a production by John Philip Kemble at Covent Garden, on January 9, 1808.

Several actors, well known to the playgoers of the eighteenth century, seem to have increased their reputation by their connection with the play; notably, Quick, as Dromio of Ephesus, and Munden, as Dromio of Syracuse. At a performance given for his benefit, Rees played Dromio of Ephesus opposite Munden, imitating the latter's voice and manner closely. In Kemble's production, Munden held his usual rôle, with Blanchard, who was considerably shorter and could not possibly be mistaken for him, playing Dromio of Ephesus.

The most singular chapter in the history of *The Comedy of Errors* opened on December 11, 1819, when

the play was given at Covent Garden as an opera, 'in
five acts with Alterations, Additions, and with Songs,
Duets, Glees, and Chorusses, Selected entirely from the
Plays, Poems and Sonnets of Shakespeare.' This
singular production drew together an assortment of
Shakespeare's lyrics which included several songs from
As You Like It, two of the Sonnets, the 'Willow Song'
from *Othello,* and 'St. Withold footed thrice the Wold'
from *Lear.* In order to introduce all these songs of
diverse nature into *The Comedy of Errors,* the reviser
found that 'a few additional scenes and passages were
absolutely necessary'; and he set himself to his task
with as little regard for the expense of scenery as
for the text of Shakespeare. The last scene of the
third act opened with a magnificent set including
mountains 'whose tops are covered with snow,' a river,
and a rustic bridge. Horns were heard without, and
the purpose of the set was shortly disclosed by the
entrance of a hunting party, who sang 'a quartetto and
chorus from *Love's Labour's Lost.*'

'This literary murder,' says Genest, 'was committed
by Reynolds'; and he goes on to assure the author that
'the only sentiments which the real friends of Shakespeare can feel towards him are indignation at his
attempt, and contempt for the bungling manner in
which he has executed it.' Other friends of Shakespeare than Genest may well feel a little chagrin at
the thought that this unpalatable gallimaufry was
presented twenty-seven times in its first season and
was frequently revived, and that Frederick Reynolds
was so encouraged by his success with *The Comedy of
Errors* that he continued his assaults upon the plays,
presenting operatic versions of *Twelfth Night, The
Tempest, Two Gentlemen of Verona,* and *The Merry
Wives of Windsor.* It may be said, in extenuation of
the sins of the theatre-going public, that Reynolds
could avail himself of the services of those 'lovely sing-
ing actresses,' Mrs. Stephens and Maria Tree, who

acted Adriana and Luciana in his production of the *Errors*.

A revival of the play, not in its strange operatic garb, was given by Samuel Phelps, who played it at Sadler's Wells in November, 1855, and again in January, 1856. This production was followed, in the spring of 1864, on the occasion of the Shakespeare Tercentenary, by an interesting performance given at the Princess' Theatre and through the provinces. The play was acted continuously without the fall of the curtain, and with a strikingly beautiful stage mounting. The two brothers, Charles and Harry Webb, played the two Dromios, giving an extraordinary interpretation, which kept the audience in bewilderment by their similarity in appearance and actions. At a performance by the Webbs in Liverpool in this year, S. B. Bancroft acted Antipholus of Syracuse and John Hare appeared as Dr. Pinch.

In January, 1883, J. S. Clarke, the brother-in-law of Edwin Booth, put on a 'pictorial revival,' for which Lewis Wingfield designed the setting and costumes. On this occasion, Clarke and Harry Paulton, who acted the two Dromios, seem to have secured their comic effect by emphasizing the differences between the twin slaves as much as the similarity. In more recent years, the play has been included in the repertory of the Benson company, for their London season in 1905, with F. R. Benson as Antipholus of Syracuse and the two Dromios by George Weir and Arthur Whitby. The most recent revival, on the London stage, was a performance given as a curtain-raiser to a production of *The Bells* at the Savoy Theatre during the summer of 1924. The comedy was played very rapidly and was well received.

Outside of England, *The Comedy of Errors* has had no very noteworthy history. When performed at the Künstlertheater in Munich, in September, 1910, under the direction of Max Reinhardt of Berlin, the play

was referred to as 'a novelty'; though it is to be said
that the same authority describes the production as
'the culminating success of an artistic and clever
management' (*Athenæum*, October 1, 1910). In
America, the play was not acted until 1804, when a
production was given at the Park Theatre, New York,
on May 25. The most notable revival in this country
was that of William H. Crane and Stuart Robson in
1878. Robson and Crane, who acted the two Dromios,
were not in the least alike in appearance, but, with the
aid of dress and make-up, they achieved a remarkable
resemblance. 'Intellectual vacuity was expressed in
a blank stare, a rocking gait, fingers sucked or tapped
and pressed together, and irresolute swaying, while
voices raised in whimpering protest or bleating in
appeal called answering laughter from the audience.'

APPENDIX C

The earliest known text of *The Comedy of Errors* is that of the First Folio of 1623.

By permission of the Oxford University Press, the text of the present edition is based upon that of the Oxford Shakespeare, edited by the late W. J. Craig. Departures from Craig's text are indicated below.

1. So far as possible, the stage directions of the Folio have been restored. Necessary additions have been inserted in square brackets.

2. Punctuation and spelling have been normalized to accord with modern English practice; e.g. courtesan, almanac (instead of courtezan, almanack). In the case of the words murther, burden, burthen, etc., the actual form employed by the Folio has been retained.

3. The following alterations in Craig's text have been introduced, readings of the present edition standing before the colon, while those of Craig follow it. Except in the two instances indicated, these changes restore the reading of the Folio.

I. i. 15	To admit: T' admit
	87	was: were
	119	misfortunes: misfortune
	127	so: for
II. i. 110	yet the: and though
	111	and: yet
ii. 124	then: thus
	150	distain'd: unstain'd
	155	wants: want
	194	sprites: elvish sprites
	209	laughs: laugh
III. i. 106	hous'd: housed
ii. 113	that's: that is
	135	saw it: saw
IV. i. 16	end: that will I: end, that I will

56	me by: by me
iii. 24	sob: fob
66	then: thee
iv. 106	these false: those false
V. i. 70	Poisons: Poison
79	moody: moody moping
86	Hath: Have
137	Who: Whom
183	scorch: scotch
189	there: here
215	disturbed: disturb'd
242	living dead: living-dead
246	all together: altogether (F)
405	burthen ne'er: burdens ne'er (burthen are F)
408	go: joy

APPENDIX D

Comedy of Errors' with those in the 'Menæchmi.' University of Texas Studies in English, Number 5. Austin, 1925.

The most useful annotated edition of *The Comedy of Errors* that has yet appeared is that in the Arden series, edited by Henry Cunningham, London, 1907. The edition of Sir Arthur Quiller-Couch and Mr. J. Dover Wilson, for the Cambridge University Press (1922), contains an interesting, if rather imaginative, essay on 'The Copy for *The Comedy of Errors*, 1623.'

INDEX OF WORDS GLOSSED

(Figures in full-faced type refer to page-numbers)